VERSUS VERSUS

Cover image description: This book's cover features a square-shaped artwork by Polish artist, Julian Stanczak, entitled 'Concurrent Colors'. The painting creates an optical illusion of vertical moving curved lines in red and blue, giving the impression of moving waves or sand dunes. At the edges of the painting the lines thin out so that they resemble a comb effect. The painting has a darker blue framing band around it, filling the extent of the cover. The title of the anthology 'VERSUS VERSUS' is in a large red font at the top of the cover, and the subtitle, '100 POEMS BY DEAF, DISABLED & NEURODIVERGENT POETS', is in a large blue font underneath the square painting. The editor's name, Rachael Boast, is in a smaller red font beneath the subtitle.

Rachael Boast is a British writer, editor and disability advocate, navigating Ichthyosis and related conditions. She has published four collections of poetry with Picador, *Sidereal* (2011), *Pilgrim's Flower* (2013), *Void Studies* (2016) and *Hotel Raphael* (2021). Her poems have been anthologised in *Stairs and Whispers: D/deaf and Disabled Poets Write Back* (Nine Arches, 2017), *Staying Human* (Bloodaxe Books, 2020) and *100 Poems to Save the Earth* (Seren, 2021). She co-edited *The Echoing Gallery: Bristol Poets and Art in the City* (Redcliffe Press, 2013) and *The Caught Habits of Language: An Entertainment for W.S. Graham for Him Having Reached One Hundred* (Donut Press, 2018). Her anthology *Versus Versus: 100 Poems by Deaf, Disabled & Neurodivergent Poets* (Bloodaxe Books, 2025) is a Poetry Book Society Recommendation. She is a Fellow of the Royal Society of Literature.

VERSUS VERSUS

100 POEMS BY DEAF, DISABLED & NEURODIVERGENT POETS

Edited by Rachael Boast

BLOODAXE BOOKS

Introduction, selection and notes © Rachael Boast 2025.
Poems copyright © rights holders:
see Publication Acknowledgements, 200-06.

ISBN: 978 1 78037 731 5

First published in the UK in 2025 by
Bloodaxe Books Ltd,
Eastburn,
South Park,
Hexham,
Northumberland NE46 1BS

www.bloodaxebooks.com
For further information about Bloodaxe titles
please visit our website and join our mailing list
or write to the above address for a catalogue.

Supported using public funding by
**ARTS COUNCIL
ENGLAND**

Cover design: Neil Astley & Pamela Robertson-Pearce.

Printed in Great Britain by Bell & Bain Limited, 303 Burnfield Road,
Thornliebank, Glasgow G46 7UQ, Scotland, on acid-free paper
sourced from mills with FSC chain of custody certification.

CONTENTS

INTRODUCTION

This anthology takes its title from a phrase found in the work of Brooklyn-born artist Jean-Michel Basquiat, known for merging text and image in his work and using repurposed materials such as planks of wood, window and door frames, whatever could be sourced from the city street, a fitting backdrop for his exploration of dichotomies and social frictions. The title was chosen for its vitality and assertiveness, how it playfully repeats itself, relishing in paradox but ultimately going beyond, transcending the pitching of one thing against another in favour of a bringing together. In addition, there is also the distant etymology of 'versus' as past participle of the Latin *vertere*, to 'turn' or 'change', and its relation to both the agrarian image of the turn of the plough at the end of a furrow and to poetry – a line that 'turns' to give way to the next line.

That the opposite of being 'versus', or against something, is being affirming, or perhaps being together in concurrence, is a good way of describing the kind of space this book intends to create – a space for nondisabled people to engage with a selection of outstanding poems; for deaf, disabled and neurodivergent people to enjoy companionship; and for some to play a part in opening up the conversation around deafness, disability and neurodivergence. Anyone advocating in this field of study will tell you that this conversation has been taking place for decades yet has still not reached far enough to find that turning point where we might acknowledge just how unenlightened our cultures are, and seek redress. Poetry can have a special role in addressing these issues.

A number of poetry anthologies have been published in recent years providing a platform for deaf, disabled or neurodivergent writers. Literary Journals and magazines have also provided a platform for discussion over the past decade or so with special themed issues and folios. Details of these can be found in the reading list housed at the end of this anthology. Without the publication and availability of these books and journals, and of the extensive individual advocacy work behind them, it would have been more difficult to assemble this anthology's contributors together, and so I want to acknowledge those individuals, editors and organisations that have enabled *Versus Versus* to be international in scope.

This volume is intended to be a selection, not a compendium. A larger book would not have worked for several reasons, not least the physical encumbrance. While my decision to keep to one hundred poets involved tough decisions, it also enables a distinctive and curated journey through the material, for each poem to have its due space, while also offering pointers to further reading and wider engagement.

I am very conscious of the under-reporting of deafness, disability and neurodivergence within particular countries and communities and of the poets it was not possible to include here because of the dangers of declaring those identities and the impact that might have on individuals and their families and friends. I hope we can hasten a time when an anthology such as this could be liberated from the hindrance of prejudice still so rife around the world. Contributing to that prejudice is how the 'medical model' of disability (the prevalent outlook for most nondisabled people) has a habit of pathologising deafness, disability or neurodivergence – and by that what is emphasised is a lack or loss of something and an emphasis either on fixes and cures or, in many cases, societal abandonment. There is little acknowledgement that prejudicial attitudes, flawed interpretations of value, eugenicist legacies, lack of access and provision, low income or no income, are a key factor in what actually disables people, creating a vicious cycle, fuelled by pathos. Pathos arises out of a colossal misunderstanding. The narrative is so often that deafness, disability or neurodivergence has to be framed within a narrative of tragedy, that it merits an outpouring of pity, whereas the real tragedy is ignorance. How to look after yourself better as a deaf, disabled or neurodivergent person must necessarily include turning pathos on its head in a spirit of resistance.

In the pages of this book the reader will find just such resistance: acts of creative vigour, of community and warmth; poems which call out 'the ableist gaze', challenging presumptions and stereotypes; love poems, pain poems, diagnosis or misdiagnosis poems; poems addressing the coronavirus pandemic; manifestos, humour, self-care, acts of witness and solidarity; war poems, poems addressing the impacts of industrial pollution and the climate emergency; poems that expose the consequences of colonial legacies, histories of land-grabbing and exploitation. There are poems which satirise some of the common and clichéd misapprehensions of deafness, disability or neurodivergence – such as equating blindness, deafness, amputation or mental illness with loss, or fetishising visible difference, or going the other way and equating these identities with super-power, heroism or special gift. In addition, there are poems which address policies and practices, political or social, historical and current, designed to cause disadvantage or damage. These poems remind us to learn about the past and to consider how toxic legacies are continued.

The terminology of 'deaf', 'disabled' or 'neurodivergent' is culturally specific, neither settled nor definitive, and not everyone chooses to use these descriptors. Most of the work included here is by contemporary writers, from across the age spectrum – from community elders to emerging authors – writing in a range of styles and from varying traditions. Also included is a sampling of historical poets: Abdullah al-Baradouni, Riyad al-Saleh al-Hussein, Paul Celan, Badr Shākir al-Sayyāb, Shiki Itsuma, Osip Mandelstam, William Soutar and Hàn Mặc Tử. A sample of poems by authors impacted by war, conflict and displacement, whether physically or in terms of mental health, was likewise indispensable in opening an appreciation of the broader context for this anthology,

given the intrinsic policy of military forces to create disability –
and indeed weaponise it – to weaken, demean and dehumanise.

This introductory note is not the place to talk in detail about
how we need to transform the narrative, how deafness, disability
and neurodivergence are still very much marginalised for being
little understood. The poems in this anthology have the privilege
of doing exactly that, in surprising and satisfying ways. Aside
from the poetry collections, journals and online magazines from
which these poems are sourced, many of the authors featured,
along with their contemporaries, have written and published
children's books, fiction, memoir, hybrid poetry and art work,
essays and other non-fiction. A number of those publications are
listed at the back of this book within the biographical notes.

This anthology has been curated to generate an encounter with
a selection of leading deaf, disabled and neurodivergent poets,
allowing for unsung realities to be brought into fuller public
consciousness.

RACHAEL BOAST

ACKNOWLEDGEMENTS

This anthology was prepared with the help of an Advocacy and Advisory Panel – Karthika Naïr, Chisom Okafor and Daniel Sluman. The panel were essential in the preparation of this book, bringing their knowledge, expertise and creativity to bear through email conversations, voice notes and online meetings. I extend my heartfelt thanks for their contributions, support, encouragement and friendship.

Thanks also to those who have been in community with this project: San Alland, Raymond Antrobus, Khairani Barokka, Anthony Vahni Capildeo, Andy Ching, Meg Day, Andy Jackson, Aaron Kent, Petra Kuppers, Pamela Robertson-Pearce, Clare Pollard and Nuala Watt. Thanks to all the contributors, translators, publishers and author estates for allowing work to be included.

Many thanks to Neil Astley and all the team at Bloodaxe Books for their dedication to this project. I couldn't have asked for a more enthusiastic publisher.

And many thanks also to the RNIB and Scottish Sensory Hub for their assistance.

Grateful thanks to The Royal Society of Literature and the judges of the 2023 Literature Matters Awards for selecting this anthology as one of the winning entries.

KHANDO LANGRI

Medicine mantra for the road

I

again
we begin with that
undertone of the universe;   (om)
that sound which renders
silence a parable   (do away with the)
pain of illness
the dust which rubs
the body raw, each speck
a tooth   (unbodied).

II

go lightly   (like this)
to the frayed edges of place;
unspool the map
picking
its threads   (apart)
for rope

JEN CAMPBELL

First Thing, I Am a Forest

When I wake up and I cannot see, I reach
for the hyaluronic acid on my bedside

table – hoping that I do not accident-
ally knock it floorwards, hear it

roll beneath the bedframe, on and on
into the graveyard of a spider-queen.

See, there are webs stuck to my eyelids,
too; sewn shut to keep the ghosts out of this

temporary bone house. I've begun to wear
a rain jacket in an attempt to escape

this weathering. Like an owl might
hold an umbrella, or a tree might

fold itself inside a greenhouse:
an origami giantess. And I guess

that when I wake up and I cannot see,
I imagine that our mattress is the earth of some

far-flung kingdom – one where, good god,
it is rude to stand and stare, and so everyone there

just pretends they are a tree. How wild,
this ancient forestry. How bone dry,

                    I blink

to let the rain in; wait
to see   a somewhat scratched-out sky.

STEPHEN KUUSISTO

Night Seasons

Up late, reading alone,
I feed printed pages
Into the Kurzweil scanner,
An electronic reader
For the blind.

Randomly now
I take books from my shelves,
Open the mysterious volumes,
And lay them flat on the machine.
I can't say
What's coming next –
I wait in perfect silence
For the voice to begin,
This synthetic child
Reading to an old man.

The body, stalled,
Picks fragments,
Frottage,
Scraps of paper,
Whatever comes.

Pico della Mirandola,
Egyptian love poems,
Essene communes beside the Red Sea,
Paavo Haavikko's 'König Harald'...

An old professor,
Bitter at the graceful way

The poets have
Of gathering terms
Inexactly,
Told me, 'The poets are fools.
They read
Only in fragments.'

I'm the fool
Of the night seasons,
Reading anything, *anything*.
When daylight comes
And you see me on the street
Or standing for the bus,
Think of the Greek term
Entelechy,
Word for soul and body
Constructing each other
After dark.

LATEEF McLEOD

I Am Too Pretty for Some 'Ugly Laws'

I am not supposed to be here
in this body,
here
speaking to you.
My mere presence
of erratic moving limbs
and drooling smile
used to be scrubbed
off the public pavement.

Ugly laws used to be
on many U.S. cities law books
beginning in Chicago in 1867
stating that 'any person who is
diseased, maimed, mutilated,
or in any way deformed
so as to be an unsightly or disgusting object,
or an improper person to be allowed
in or on the streets, highways, thoroughfares,
or public places in this city,
shall not therein or thereon
expose himself to public view,
under the penalty of $1 for each offense.'

Any person who looked like me
was deemed disgusting
and was locked away
from the eyes of the upstanding citizens.

I am too pretty for some Ugly Laws,
too smooth to be shut in.
Too smart and eclectic
for any box you put me in.
My swagger is too bold
to be swept up in these public streets.

You can stare at me all you want.
No cop will buss in my head
and carry me away to an institution.
No doctor will diagnose me
a helpless invalid with an incurable disease.
No angry mob with clubs and torches
will try to run me out of town.
Whatever you do,
my roots are rigid
like a hundred-year-old tree.
I will stay right here
to glare at your ugly face too.

JOHN LEE CLARKE

At the Holiday Gas Station

Near the Naked Juices I passed
A man my fingers walking
Across his back he turned and held up
A box said what
Might this be I said oh
You're tactile too what's your name
He said William Amos Miller I said
I thought you were born in 1872 he said so
You know who I am yes you're the man
Who journeyed to the center of Earth
In your mind he smiled on my arm said do
You know that the Earth also journeyed
To the center of my mind I said
I never thought of that he asked
Again about the box I shook it sniffed
Said Mike and Ike is it fruit
He inquired not exactly well
I think I shall have an apple wait
You haven't paid oh
My money nowadays is no money he pushed
Outside we walked across the ice
To the intersection he made to go across
Wait you can't go across we have to wait
For help oh help he said crouching
Until our hands touched the cold ground
He said I said we said we see
With our hands I jumped up and said you're the man

TITO RAJARSHI MUKHOPADHYAY
Misfit

There was the earth, turning and turning.
The stars receded, as if
Finding no wrong with anything.

Birds flew by all morning –
The sky lit
From the earth's turning and turning.

My hands, as usual, were flapping.
The birds knew I was Autistic;
They found no wrong with anything.

Men and women stared at my nodding;
They labelled me a Misfit
(A Misfit turning and turning).

And then I was the wind, blowing.
Did anyone see my trick?
I found no wrong with anything.

Somewhere a wish was rising,
Perhaps from between my laughing lips.
Why stop turning and turning
When right can be found with everything?

LINDA HOGAN

When the Body

When the body wishes to speak, she will
reach into the night and pull back the rapture of this growing root
which has no faith in the other planets of the universe,
but her feet have walked in the same bones
of the ancestors over long trails,
leaving behind the oldest forest. They walk on the ghosts
of all that has gone before them, not just plant, but animal, human,
the bones of the ones who left their horses to drink with them
at the spring running through earth's mortal body
which has much to tell about what happened that day.

When the body wishes to speak from the hands, it tells
how it pulled children back from death and it remembers every detail,
washing the children's bodies, legs, bellies, the delicate lips of the girl,
the vulnerable testicles of the son,
that future my people brought out of the river
in a spring freeze. That is only part of the story of hands
that touched our future.

This all started so simply, just a body with so much to say,
one with the hum of her own life in a quiet room,
one of the root growing, finding a way through stone,
one not remembering nights with men and guns,
the ragged clothing and broken bones of my body.

Let's go back to the hands, the thumb that makes us human,
but don't other creatures use tools and lift what they need,
intelligent all, like the crows here, one making a cast of earth clay
for the broken wing of the other, remaining
until it healed, then breaking the clay to fly away together.

I would do that, too,
since a human can make no claims
better than any other, especially without wings,
only hands that don't know these intelligent lessons.

Still, I think of the willows
made into a fence and even cut, they began to root and leaf,
then tore off the wires as they grew.

A human does throw off bonds if she can, if she tries, if it's possible.
The body is so finely a miracle of its own, created of the elements
of anything that lived on earth
where everything that was
still is.

JANET FRAME

I Take into My Arms More Than I Can Bear To Hold

I take into my arms more than I can bear to hold
I am toppled by the world
a creation of ladders, pianos, stairs cut into the rock
a devouring world of teeth where even the common snail
eats the heart out of a forest
as you and I do, who are human, at night

yet still I take into my arms more than I can bear to hold

JANE BURN

An Evanescent Garden

(after 'Horse's Skull with Pink Rose' by Georgia O'Keeffe, 1931)

This bone has become an Eden. Picked clean
of unnecessary flesh, it is spared the tangling of thought,
the seeing of what cannot be unseen. Petals flush
upon its hollow skull – settle above its vanished life,
soften its truth with gentle bloom. Perfume fills the barren cave –
attar where eyes once turned like patient wheels,
marrow of scent replacing scarlet cells. And yet,

the head is plucked and without root, cannot keep its perfect skin,
will parch and dwindle, wither like a dead mare's pelt.
The forehead, smooth as a psalter's page is wreathed
by wings of green. The horse has forgotten its glorious self.
Instead of memory, an oubliette.
Instead of worry, light.
Instead of knowledge, air.

AIREA D. MATTHEWS

Eviction

(for Wisława)

As if I created this
pyramid of obey and exist.
Between the breathturn stares
of others, also exiled, and those
who called me all but my name,
I nearly forgot that I could,
unlike Lot's wife, glance back
for the answers – some threads
of truth where memory faltered.
In sooth, that snake was not a reptile.
The fruit of good and evil
was a flower of wasps, not an apple.
I was less inbred rib – more accurately,
unbred. Love was often anguished and
paradise looked like anybody's
milkweed garden. I didn't
beg Adam's pardon and never
asked *why me, o Lord?* No
proverbs would suffice when
genesis is what is and was what
was. I looked, instead, to the present
as the past cracked underfoot,
lowered into riverbeds. The waters
rose below and leagues above flaming
vines enveloped the stairs to heaven
glister by glister. Due east, fly ash
blanketed each morning glory
I named in light, pocked
the night phlox perfumed distant

moons ago. I vowed from the eye
of that reckoning, fates among
Eves would not be the same:

If one sister is silenced into salt
without body that remembers,
then I will batter my cymbals
bearing witness for us both
with what body still remains.

CHISOM OKAFOR

In another life, I am twenty-two, gifted and curious

and dreaming of fleeing the world, while perched on the transom
of a stallion of the sea, breathing stale evening air off the waterline, and
an entanglement of sodium chloride and ancient seawood.
The boy on the other side is waiting, arms outstretched
as though to receive a prodigal advancing
to the interlocking welcome of an embrace.
Worn by the ways of the sea, I have mastered
the art of smearing my sternum with white and green watermarks
and this is the year of my first diagnosis, and I'm pressing
a miniature paintbrush to my chest, tracing the shape of a heart,
feeble with cardiomegaly, and whispering
the words of the scriptures into it:
Talitha cumi. Talitha cumi. Feeble girl, rise up. Rise up.
And I'm thinking of what happens to the heart when its vessel –
an entire body – is immersed in water
and left to slouch against the rippling music of immersion.
I am thinking of the calculus of bodies, the time between Point X and
    Point Y –
time between immersion and the bottom of the sea –
the exquisite mathematics of drowning.

ADA LIMÓN

The Endlessness

At first I was lonely, but then I was
curious. The original fault was that I could
not see the lines of things. My mother could.
She could see shapes and lines and shadows,
but all I could see was memory, what had been
done to the object before it was placed on
the coffee table or the nightstand. I could sense
that it had a life underneath it. Because
of this, I thought I was perhaps bad at seeing. Even
color was not color, but a mood. The lamp was
sullen, a candlestick brooding and rude with its old
wax crumbling at its edges, not flame, not a promise
of flame. How was I supposed to feel then? About
moving in the world? How could I touch anything
or anyone without the weight of all of time shifting
through us? I was not, or I did not think I was, making
up stories; it was how the world was, or rather it is how
the world is. I've only now become better at pretending
that there are edges, boundaries, that if I touch
something it cannot always touch me back.

HEIDI ANDREA RESTREPO RHODES
A Small Disunified Theory

We've gone pale all over, a capital drain
through which forever is stripped of its *or* –
manufactured selection reduced to fever.
The fetish of radiant tragedies, handmaidens
dressed in collateral adjectives. Aren't we

rendered a menagerie? A diluted
zoomorphic palette, our racked bodies, *kittens*
& rabbits & sunsets & sordid red satin
goddesses. The altar a pedestaled cage. Our hair
feeds the fibrous needs of the heavens. Queens

of miserable. It says all this here, in the doctor's
script, his terrible cursive. Patriarchy's bloat
& interlock. Exploit & cramp.

We ailment & scorn. Barely a sign, these
broken hearts, broken bones, broken lungs. Caught
in centuries of wound, ever after
of the world. Its rhythms of subjugation.
The body is simply an extension, a spasm

of the wound. The world. The choral refrain
of experts: it's all in our heads
in our heads   in our heads.

The choral refrain of despots
& hoarders of gain, of gatekeepers &
too many men: it's all in our heads
in our heads   in our heads   in our
heads. Let the body speak (of its illnesses, its

dispossessions), declare its stolen. Let the body
say it for you. A crown-to-heel testimony,
inflammatory indeed.

Summon the memory, the nebulous
conditions of our devastation. Summon
the acute & chronic aftermath. The throb
& burn of aperture & rift. Drastic shapes
call for what will be deemed drastic measures:

from the outside, orchestral noise abounds.
We know how to handle each other's
blood. How to butter our bread.

I learn the names of your mothers, you mine.

Study the sounds of your dispossessions,
the pace of your pulse under upheaval,
laughter masking stiff tissue form. I your
& you mine, I your & you mine.

Our wounds, our bodies & their becomings.
A fetal universe in lambent hungers.

A snow early & long in the arms, but here
we are, coruscating against invasion,
vining our way up through it.
A mess of aching limbs devoted to the light.

Staggering, isn't it?

How improbable we are.

_____

This poem's title, italicised lines, and various words and images are sourced
from or riffing on Leslie Jamison's 2014 essay, 'A Grand Unified Theory of
Female Pain'.

SANDRA ALLAND

having been

sent the means to the past,
they are as she now; looking on.
Men dip the warden of the US, and sexual
pursuant is this, is different: the means to
irresponsibly *you know* their space.
The soul can be either flamenco or duty.

Will the abled. I lately
juicy in their many years. You're good as the elegantly.
I always but but but, then say you're
the bull. Gone.

Want to lose the Baby, though. You can then be but actual.

From 'I'll go on', the play of its own is still
femme. And I go. I've lately means
to be an ape of the year.

ANDY JACKSON

Song not for you

(after 'Das Lied des Zwerges' – The song of the dwarf – Rainer Maria Rilke)

Crooked blood, stunted hands, cripple,
out of place – uncanny how small
thoughts can be, while I'm incomparable,
only a dwarf because the so-called average
person is taller. You ought
to just walk on by, but don't. Ever thought
how inflated you must look from this

height? When I walk or shop, I'm inspiring,
it seems. *Fantastic to see you getting*
out, you say, as you imagine waking
up in my body, the courage
you'd need not to kill yourself, stat.
How do you live with that?
That's me wondering back,
distractedly eating (wow!) a sandwich.

In my home, I've made it so I come
face to face with the cupboards and oven, belonging
as we all want it. I sleep in my bed (some-
times alone). At work, my cubicle's longer
and wider than yours. True,
this isn't much of a song –
but then it never was meant for you.

LEAH LAKSHMI PIEPZNA-SAMARASINHA

Crip fairy godmother

(for Maya Chinchilla)

Hi, baby crip
I know, you feel like a ton of bricks just hit you. They did.
But I'm your crip fairy godmother
and I'm here to tell you what's going to happen.
I hate to say it, but it's a cheat sheet called, they mostly don't care about us

Because this is exactly what's going to happen:
Your able-bodied friends will stop calling.
It's going to be real cute for a minute,
but then there will be other things to look at on Instagram
They're going to wish you a 'speedy recovery'
and they will be so surprised when there is neither
speed   or a recovery.
They will say, 'oh, you're not disabled, sweetie, don't call yourself that.'
They will laugh uncomfortably when you state simple facts about your
    body
They will tell you to hurry up
every way they can
with every deep sigh, every *it's fine,*
every time they'll walk ahead of you so fast
they don't even notice you're gone.
There will be expectations of gratitude!
There will be, 'Hope you feel better soon!'

Most of all there's this:
they will forget you
You have to know this, they will forget you,
over and over again.

They will forget you use a chair   They will forget you use a cane.
They will forget you think in flowers   They will forget that you're Deaf,
and they will think they're doing you a favor
by forgetting your disability
because that means you get to be human, like them.
If they can't forget these things
they are going to forget
that you exist.

They're gonna take your sick personally
I mean very personally   I mean you are in a wheelchair *at* them,
I mean you are puking and shitting for hours *at* them,
I mean you *did this*, by which I mean, you got disabled, to get at them
because they, the abled, are the centre of the world
and when you continue to exist
you're gonna be a rip in the fabric of their universe.
You're going to give a shit about things you never cared about before
and they're going to be so grateful
they aren't you

They will stop calling
They will care about you but not other disabled people because we are
    still losers
They will have absolutely no idea of the hurt they cause with every
    syllable
but you will.

I know this sucks
but I'm your crip fairy godmother and I'm here to give you some
    important information straight
This is not in any pamphlet the hospital will send you home with
its operating instructions. I mean to save your life
with what I was taught in the secret guild of other sickos
with what I learned the hard way

Dear baby crip,
it's not all bad news,
because here's what's also going to happen
It's a magic spell I'm calling into existence
It's Defense against the White Able-Bodied Arts time!
This is crip Hogwarts with none of the racism or heteronormativity!
This is all our lightning scars on our foreheads glowing, not just one
    special white boy's!

Because here's what's also going to happen,
after they leave
after nothing   and everything
happens on your rebel body's schedule
You will discover
that you
do
not
give
a fuck.
You will discover that they bore the hell out of you
right next to them breaking your heart.

It will probably take you years
to begin to maybe not hate yourself
but I invoke that you will
This is a magic spell,
because we write the future with our bodies every day
that you make it
and make more than you could imagine
You will gain a wild pack of crips
sharing vicodin, hearing aid hookups, favourite terps, the shared ramp
the inside scoop on the lexapro, the link to the beloved breathing mask.

You will drool   type   stim   limp
and shake with joy
I invoke that you will move as slow and weird as you want
and others will roll and limp with you in a wild pack of slowness

You will gain skill in learning to not predict the future
You will learn every magic trick
to shape-shift pain
You become an alchemist
and you are better than
any of the most boring neurotypicals in the world

Didn't Lauren Olamina, that crip, say:

All successful life is
Adaptable,
Opportunistic,
Tenacious,
Interconnected, and
Fecund.
Understand this.
Use it.
Shape God.[1]

Shape god
You, you are god

Disability is adaptive, interconnected, tenacious, voracious, slutty,
    silent, raging,
life giving

---

[1] Octavia Butler, 'Earthseed: Book of the Living, verse 19', *Parable of the Sower*
(New York: Four Walls Eight Windows, 1993).

We are crip Earthseed
but we are not going anywhere
You are not an individual health defect
You are a systematic war battalion
You come from somewhere
You are a we
We know shit they'll need to know
We know shit they have no idea of
We have survived a million things they said would kill us
We prove them all wrong
Even death is different here
not a failure
but a glittery cosmos.

What can I do?

I can breathe sky into the spaces of my spasming spine
I can eat Fritos and watch an entire series on Netflix with no shame
I organise my whole community without ever leaving my bed
I can show you how to make a ramp out of some styrofoam and a hot dog
I can run a million miles a second panic attack wired for sound
I am a hyperempath like Lauren Olamina
I can run this whole show tapping emails on my phone with my forehead
I can jump off a bridge and not fall
I regrow my neural pathways into the future
I XFemme
I can survive
I bliss
I can make sure we all make it
I can see my vulnerability
not as a crime

So tell me.

What
can you do?
What
are the magic tricks
you will teach me
that I don't even know yet,
that will be
what saves
my life

HOSHINO TOMIHIRO

筆を噛む

筆を噛み砕きたい
時がある
槍のように
突きたてたい
時もある
さまざまな思いが
風のように　過ぎて
花を見ている

HOSHINO TOMIHIRO

Chewing My Pen

Sometimes
I want to pulverise my pen between my teeth.
Sometimes
I want to seize it like a spear
and impale things with it.
Various thoughts
blow through me
while I'm looking at flowers.

translated from the Japanese by John Newton Webb

RODDY LUMSDEN

Against Complaint

(after the Yoruba)

Though the amaryllis sags and spills
so do those my wishes serve, all along the town.
And yes, the new moon, kinked there in night's patch,
tugs me so – yet I can't reach to right the slant.
And though our cat pads past without a tail, some
with slinking tails peer one-eyed at the dawn, some
with eyes are clawless, some with sparking claws
contain no voice with which to sing
of foxes gassing in the lane.
                           Round-shouldered pals
parade smart shirts, while my broad back supports
a scrubby jumper, fawn or taupe.
                           The balding English
air their stubble, while some headless hero sports
a feathered hat. I know a man whose thoroughbred
grazes in his porch for want of livery.
There are scholars of Kant who can't find Kent
on the map, and men of Kent who cannot
fathom Kant.
               We who would polish off a feast have lain
late in our beds, our bellies groaning, throats on fire.
We who'd drain a vat of wine have drunk
our own blood for its sting.
                           Each of us in tatters flaunts
one treasured garment flapping in the wind.

44

KERRI SHYING

and bulbul means heart

songbirds   woke me
this morning   absent   the alarm
no wonder I forget things
I look down
into a clothes morass
see my brain pill
nestling there
a small synaptic fowl
doing   not much good
to torn pyjama pants
all of us who take them
wonder
why make a pill so small   to treat
the loss of feeling   in your hands
sometimes the skull
is a bone cup
holding words
on paper slips
my big dumb hands go diving
in Awabakal
bulbul means heart

NAOMI ORTIZ

Epicenter

Body
ground zero
    for how we are instructed to control the world

Limitlessness is the goal
    Tap mountain spine
dig deeper to pierce vein
    Bulldozers crush, pinch, scrape, screech
compress rock into cactus flesh
    cover sheltered baby cub burrow
Siphon riches from cattle
    shoulder to shoulder in pens
Efficient production ends in abundant effluent

Body is to straddle
    home known through sour, sweet, salty
and a reality sold to us as smooth, pale, infinite
    Pump cortisol to do it all but
shame curdles the milked effort

To have a body is to whisper
    confessions of desire
Skeleton compound mineral rich
    organs fluid function
To live is to be bound by what cannot be overcome
    learn to follow body's lead

Bodies dream, wake, move, fall
      consent to touch
exert boundaries in
      yes, yass, YES
or, *No, not tonight*

Bodies host life
      bacteria dwells in eyebrows, guts, tongues
Cells regenerate for function
      Choice is chemical reaction dependent
Eyes dilate – foot pushes brake
      for roadrunner
as they streak across the pavement
      lizard tail swings from beak

Mestize body knits together borders
      learns to use thighs, instead of words, to grip on to parent hips
Hold tight above the quake of
      their hands busy tracing the void of everything left behind
Nursed with tales of loss and liberation as two sides of one

Disabled body inhabits a valley having tested the edge
      Where cane, wheel, words tipped off the ledge
To live with holes, rips, stains
      is to let life wait for now
To lay down and rest

MEG DAY

It Must Still Be Summer

(after a line by Nikky Finney)

because the tent goes up easy
in the blue grass & we loiter
past sundown without sleeves,
the sunset one thing we can watch
that won't require captioning
& isn't each other. What did you say
then, hand cupped to my ear
as if it would send more
than winter across my arm?
What did I believe I knew
of language in that moment
before everything about me
became true? I followed you
into the dark like a vowel: a train
disappearing into a tunnel,
a tunnel at the end of a light.
It's night in the tent & my eyes
can't help but deny my ears,
so it's my hands that go dowsing
for sound: the push-broom sweep
of our sleeping bags & the hourglass
sand of their slow unzip. I catch
your lip in the gold leaf glare
of your neighbor's third shift
headlights, wet road rumble in my hips
& yellow cymbal flash-bang
through your hair. I don't care
how it happened – only that it did.
One minute an eternity with you

tracing the bones of my face
with your read-along finger,
mouthing me out (quiet
common mispronunciation
I still let slide between my thighs
at the right octave). Another
& you are all whicker, flank, soft
muzzle in my palm. What makes
a woman who is barely a woman
move like this? What secret
grammar do you know? I feed apple
fingers past eager lips smacking
on THIRTEEN, plus one, the heat
of you sucking at the M
of my name sign, my girl scout
promise. What part of your body
isn't saying my name? Say it again.
Say it louder. This is the last night
of my life when hands remain
only one kind of mouth. Whose tongue
is this & where did you learn it? What made
you invent a new chord – then made me
play it like a siren for a three-alarm fire –
summon new gods with their good names
hot at the reed of my jaw like some kind
of symphony disarmed of melody?
All these questions & the answer
right there at the end of my arm.

ERICA MENA

from **Featherbone**

The featherbone shift, slip shallow wrack, shucked in veinway crush:
Predatory.   Steelfever body, oily-eyed slit   the featherbone split.
Descent.   In bonesplit crack, in featherslip fuse,   mutation
all blue   all sky   wrench the featherbone   in body ascend.

                                        'There is so much more sky – '

Stripped, slick and sanguine with the featherbone fuse, liminal
and splash, not end but apparatus masking the crack
of the featherbone. And why not transform in the scorch? Waxblood
    and sear;
dizzy rip and sweep of air through bone, the feather, the bone.

                                        '– so much more sky –'

The featherbone sought to root. In boneflight, in featherfall, in asphyxia
the featherbone seeks. Still. The featherbone seeks history and flight,
skinrip and slough already opaque where the featherbone sinks
its point to fleshfallow feed in shallow to marrow to hollow.

                                        '– than land.'

                            —

In every other telling it fails,
the word flight on the horizon –
to burrow, to flash, to flesh, to tempt like glass in a wave and shift the
    edge.

No whisper of change,
the unsought gift, just failure and fall and that part's true. The featherbone
can't resist. You have nothing to surrender in the archback fall the
   sunsear fever
the center sucked out.

—

The framework of a bird on its back, wings untouched, still attached,
the breastbone and all the main bones of the body fleshless. If the head
has been left, the neck vertebrae will be fleshless too.

(This is not always true of very large birds, which have thicker bones.)

The wind blew open
the shattered-glass glint
a surface that doesn't reflect.

In fear the breath
and here the form took shape.

Everything is full of bone.

—

'In all the overgrown neglected places the bones are sifting down –'

PAUL CELAN

Afternoon with Circus and Citadel

In Brest, before hoops of flame,
in the tent where the tiger leapt,
there, Finite, I heard you sing,
there I saw you, Mandelstam.

The sky hung above the roadstead,
the gull hung above the crane.
What is finite sang, what is constant –
you, gunboat, are called 'Baobab'.

I saluted the tricolore
speaking a Russian word –
things lost were things not lost,
the heart was a place made fast.

translated from the German by Michael Hamburger

OSIP MANDELSTAM
'Having deprived me...'

Having deprived me of seas, of running and flying away,
and allowing me only to walk upon the violent earth,
what have you achieved? A splendid result:
you could not stop my lips from moving.

[May 1935]

translated from the Russian by Richard and Elizabeth McKane

JACK MAPANJE
Skipping Without Ropes

I will, I will skip without your rope
Since you say I should not, I cannot
Borrow your son's skipping rope to
Exercise my limbs; I will skip without

Your rope as you say, even the lace
I want will hang my neck until I die;
I will create my own rope, my own
Hope and skip without your rope as

You insist I do not require to stretch
My limbs fixed by these fevers of your
Reeking sweat and your prison walls;
I will, will skip with my forged hope;

Watch, watch me skip without your
Rope; watch me skip with my hope –
A-one, a-two, a-three, a-four, a-five
I will, a-seven, I do, will skip, a-ten,

Eleven, I will skip without, will skip
Within and skip I do without your
Rope but with my hope; and I will,
Will always skip you dull, will skip

Your silly rules, skip your filthy walls,
You weevil pigeon peas, skip your
Scorpions, skip your Excellency Life
Glory. I do, you don't, I can, you can't,

I will, you won't, I see, you don't, I
Sweat, you don't, I will, will wipe my
Gluey brow then wipe you at a stroke
I will, will wipe your horrid, stinking,

Vulgar prison rules, will wipe you all
Then hop about, hop about my cell, my
Home, the mountains, my globe as your
Sparrow hops about your prison yard

Without your hope, without your rope
I swear, I will skip without your rope, I
Declare, I will have you take me to your
Showers to bathe me where I can resist

This singing child you want to shape me,
I'll fight your rope, your rules, your hope
As your sparrow does under your super-
vision! Guards! Take us for a shower!

SARAH LUBALA

6 Errant Thoughts on Being a Refugee

1

on the worst of my days
this body is a gimcrack-vessel
no more than two lungs and
a tremor
nailed to salvaged wood

2

grief travelled with me
across the Ubangi River

i prayed love
and all her cognates
on the passage over:
libet (to please)
lips (to be needed)
lyp (to beg)

i arrived with
bruised knees
wet hair
a mouth-full of salted fish

3

i am so
hungry
hungry
hungry

for holiness
for communion
for a God you can sink
your teeth into

4

i was raised
on the Congolese-gospel
i can teach you how to forget
where you are from
to worship the wide road before you
hands open
like this:
make each palm
a letter
to the sky

5

Beni is a town
with one police station
airport
market
many graves

I should go back
my people are weeping

6

'home'
is a narrow bed

ALI COBBY ECKERMANN

Kulila

sit down sorry camp
might be one week might
be long long time

tell every little story
when the people was alive
tell every little story more

don't forget 'em story
night time tell 'em to the kids
keep every story live

don't change 'em story
tell 'em straight out story
only one way story

all around 'em story
every place we been
every place killing place

sit down here real quiet way
you can hear 'em crying
all them massacre mobs

sit down here real quiet
you can feel 'em dying
all them massacre mobs

hearts can't make it up
when you feel the story
you know it's true

tell every little story
when the people was alive
tell every little story more

might be one week now
might be long long time
sit down sorry camp

STEFFI TAD-Y

Duplex Ukol Sa Utang Na Loob

I was scared my anger meant I was unlovable.
Anger, I had nowhere to put this down.

Anger, where do I put you down?
The Tagalog word for pomegranate is Granada.

Having eaten what I can't detonate, I agonise.
I agonise over gut flora while taking photographs.

I take photographs of pine, plum, & magnolia.
The trees detonate pine, plum, & magnolia.

Without a camera, my cousin saw a child explode.
I was a child of explosion after explosion.

What does it mean to witness an explosion? Carry it home?
My roots, their ears were once children too.

Anger, I look at the water in your eyes.
I was scared my anger meant I was unlovable.

JK ANOWE

a musical malady

my head sings of a departure of all reasoning an echo
a word inside every word ready to break out i fill a book
with the word *remember* to emphasise how badly i long
to remain within the confines of memory once i was
the boy who perceived humans the only beings cap-
able of memory now i return to the awe of being

grown-up to watch a nanny goat after a morning
of grazing return to breastfeed her young my mother
who lets her back in the pen forgets her own
spouse daydreams of shutting the door on his big toe
as much as i await my father's dust-feet at the thresh
-old every dream is a plot to return from the body this
unresting we packed for but do not remember

arriving at imagine a wall & on it a painting imagine
in the painting a field any field & at its centre a grand
piano with a finger nailed to its single key blood
-dripping the only possibility of sound go back to that
wall imagined are you there now do you see it isn't
that memory a sickening we return to for music

RIYAD AL-SALEH AL-HUSSEIN

The Sleeping Boy

Before he went to war, he marched toward the bed
closed his eyes and slept...
He saw in a boyish dream
a spacious plain with galloping deer
a flock of birds
peach trees
moonlike flowers
He saw a very spacious day
and deep into the day, a man came walking
threw a bloody shirt at the child
the plain vanished, the deer perished,
the trees followed
the day disappeared...
The handsome boy said: that's okay.
He closed his eyes with his own eyes
and slept
saw twenty angels perched near him
proposed: let us eat oranges
let us play cat and mouse
I will hide on top of my bed
now find me, dear cat/angel...

....

And from the farthest sky
a bomb dropped over the handsome boy's bed
the angel flew
the cat meowed, seeing the child's finger sinking in the dirt
the handsome boy said:
That's okay, that's okay

Exhausted, he went back to bed
closed his eyes with his own eyes
and slept...
Saw in a dream
fish on the walls
a wolf swimming in a pool
a crocodile returning to the nightclub
and a woman waiting for God before the Palace of Justice.
The handsome boy cried:
I don't want to see anything
I want my mother, my bottle, my blanket.
The handsome boy said something
not that pleasing
yet not distasteful:
'long live the duck
long live the river
long live the cat
long live the trees
long live my sister, my brother
and down with the tank'...

...
...

He closed his eyes with his own eyes
and slept, once and for all

translated from the Arabic by Ibtihal Rida Mahmood

KHAIRANI BAROKKA

Tub

what digs you out with a verdigris scalpel, while a powerful blast
ignited in their latest attempt to grow lives in the dirt of your online
receipt, human blood carries all kinds of filigreed debris, coexisting
with the coffin hinges from grotesquely groping eyes panoptic that
brought you your morning kettle-hiss, faucet fiddling now, let loose,
hotness   coldness, piety, lust, bewilderment, supremacy writ into
capital, rent hikes for men oiling hair with your rainforests, corners
hiding gaspings for breath, a ladybug swatted away by a tank in
gaza, a man with down's syndrome killed with no consequences,
violet memories of neuropathic pain still imprinted on your body
you are soaking in a fluid warm enough to let it bleed out, breathe
in, deliberately feel the edges of a ghost, the heart already drawn in
pencil on your hospital radiator seven years ago, fuzzy twinges bear
on your muscle feel these deliberate, you may not bathe in kind waters
so lower your head below the surface, part your lips and scream it

URVASHI BAHUGUNA

Medical History

(after Nicole Sealey)

Alprax for my aunt's divorce. Alprax for the nights
my sister isn't coming home. Two Disprin and a glass
of lemonade for the bi-weekly headache. I have never
been pregnant, though I'm told often it buds and ebbs,
and no one ever knows. A whole pond of possibility
quietly blooming and evaporating on its own. Crepe
bandages for an old football injury. Iron supplements
monthly for dizziness from blood loss during periods.
Anti-allergy tablets for cockroaches, mould, and milk.
My mother had a knee surgery at 50 for a bone sliver
dislodged at age 15. In the 70s, no one paid attention
to breaks and scrapes. Antidepressants after heart
surgery for my grandfather. Back brace and around
the clock bed rest for one grandmother and a walker
for the other. Sleeping tablets for travel, for bad fights
before bedtime. Heart attacks on both sides of my
family tree. I have nightmares from the afternoon
the doctor suspected I might have cancer, and thrust
a probe inside me without warning. I counted from one
to a hundred after she called me very, very difficult
for screaming in pain. Forgive me if I can't complete
this history. If there are facts I don't want to record.
I tried my best to both be honest and to redirect
my punches towards the water behind the house.

RAYMOND ANTROBUS

For Tyrone Givans

The paper said *putting him in jail*
without his hearing aids was like
putting him in a hole in the ground.

There are no hymns
for deaf boys. But who can tell
we're deaf without speaking to us?

Tyrone's name was misspelled
in the HMP Pentonville prison system.
Once, I was handcuffed,

shoved into a police van. I didn't hear
the officer say why. I was saved
by my friend's mother who threw herself

in the road and refused to let the van drive away.
Who could have saved Tyrone?
James Baldwin attempted suicide

after each of his loves
jumped from bridges or overdosed.
He killed his characters, made them

kill themselves – *Rufus, Richard,*
Black men who couldn't live like this.
Tyrone, I won writing awards

bought new hearing aids and heard
my name through the walls.
I bought a signed Baldwin book.

The man who sold it to me didn't know
you, me or Baldwin.
I feel I rescued it. I feel failed.

Tyrone, the last time I saw you alive
I dropped my pen
on the staircase

didn't hear it fall but you saw and ran
down to get it, handed it to me
before disappearing, said,

you might need this.

KARTHIKA NAÏR & MARILYN HACKER
from A Different Distance

Tonight, an empire
of pain reigns over attempts
to write, think; to be.

Fall, even *summer*, graze past
ears as would submerged boulders.

RDEB – four
horseless, shapeless, ageless words –
must play first fiddle;

second, third, and last, as well,
while all others earn exile.

  – KN, 5 MAY 2020

Home becomes exile
in the punished city. Leaves
green beyond grillwork,

Nâzim Hikmet's postcard from
prison poems on the sill.

Locked-in lovers make
love until it bores them. Once,
through a hurricane

in Crete…but that was three days,
decades ago, two of us.

  – MH, 7 MAY 2020

This, decades ago,
was how I gaped at the sea.
Reaching Rue Manin,

the years sublime, suddenly –
much-younger selves drink from this

downpour of gloaming,
we gasp at the carnival
corralled within Parc

des Buttes-Chaumont. Cedar, elm,
and linden; pine, plane, and beech,

arch towards the sky.
Hazelnut and cherry trees
flaunt wanton blossoms,

and the cascades underground
serenade us from afar.

  – KN, 8 MAY 2020

From afar, but it
wasn't, thunder, rush of dark
clouds, then crash of rain,

just after I noticed, no
gates blocked the berges of the Île

Saint-Louis. No way
but, run under the torrents,
no café-shelter.

Strip off once indoors, shower.
Flu, or worse, I'm on my own.

Later, on my own,
I slice shallots and mushrooms
into olive oil

and begin to imagine
I might not cough tomorrow.

   – MH, 9 MAY 2020

Tomorrow might bring
the unknown – new foes, allies
of Taxol; blitzkrieg

within the chest; skull afire
(the mind sentinels one front

alone, these days) – but
also Philippe, bonne fée, by
the hospital doors,

strafed by showers or barraged,
joyfully, by vernal sun.

   – KN, 12 MAY 2020

WILLIAM SOUTAR

The Room

Into the quiet of this room
Words from the clamorous world come:
The shadows of the gesturing year
Quicken upon the stillness here.

The wandering waters do not mock
The pool within its wall of rock
But turn their healing tides and come
Even as the day into this room.

EREZ BITTON

You Who Cross My Path

You
who cross my path
and do not greet me
know that to me you do not exist
and therefore
when you come my way
say hello to me
and each one of you
will be my friend

translated from the Hebrew by Tsipi Keller

HÀN MẶC TỬ

Here in Vĩ Dạ Hamlet

Won't you return to Vĩ hamlet?
Where the sun shines through rows of palms,
In rich gardens as green as jade,
And bamboo groves that shield a face.

Wind parts clouds, each goes their way.
Water grows blue, while cornflowers sway.
Whose boat's docked there, just by the moon?
Will it reach home as the night ends soon?

Dream of a faraway, faraway passerby,
Whose shirt's too white for one's grasp to keep,
When the fog thickens, blurring one's sight,
Who knows whose love's still running deep?

translated from the Vietnamese by N.T. Anh

MASAOKA SHIKI

1898 Summer

Put the chair there –
where my knees
will touch the roses

translated from the Japanese by Burton Watson

EKIWAH ADLER-BELÉNDEZ

Evening Summer Rain

(for Mary Oliver)

To realise
fire and water are not enemies
   only twins knotted
in the braids of lightning;

to unlatch my mouth
   and unfurl my tongue
for the electricity
of each tingling drop –

to move toward the storm
   and be drenched by it, deliberately – is a reckless
summer act.

But you and I know why
we have been busy
   soaking the moment in
without rushing
for shelter. We hope for nothing less

than Heaven itself
plummeting down
into our bodies!

translated from the Spanish by the author

KAY ULANDAY BARRETT

Sick 4 Sick

Her body patched, swollen skin,
hair flecks gone rogue, mismatch
knees, ache knits quilt through out.
Curvature, a soft thing.

They said
if we hum close,
close enough that our chests touch,
shared breath comes from belly up,
      – that, that is *not* platonic.

                Now breathe same air, nostril kinetic
                by way of brow cleft pirouette of migraine.
                Syllables twirl temples. Strain is
                something to lull here, together.

                When nerves are ablaze, I'm told
                to be blanket. Lay my torso on hers,
                abdomen to abdomen, core to core,
                is this what a field does to a hill,

        spill it with poppies? I wait on
        her skill. How they will sigh.
        The human body is heating pad.
        Limbs bonfire, flip sheets, you can't
        reverse sick. Today we don't want to.
        Chests pulse softest lake.

Come spring we never do this again.
There's only memory of it,
how her lungs cathedral. How
I prayed there, on the ledge of inhale
sternum sacred, coughed hymn,
spasm luminescence.

Syllables stretched, muscled
          sacrament more than splay,
          us, petals in overlap
us, an ampersand
on fire.

Bournemouth

The sea tonight – so comported –
is no threat. Let us walk along the front.
Let us ponder the Flood,
my imaginary friend. We've been,

so far, so scrupulous – yet what
comes of it? But the sea itself is innocent.
And the front, too – utterly benign.
Place your hand in mine,

for I am afraid of my own mind.
How it turns. How it folds itself
over and over – O my endless, sentient
serviette! It will not hold water,

the doctor said. And I don't do God.
Forgive me, Mrs Lightband. I am
lost – even if this proven, human fact.
And I want only to walk with you,

as each star bleeds so long, and breaks
to each final point. And my tears
will be nothing new, and the stars –
our startlers – the stars impossibly accrue.

THERESE ESTACION
The ABG (Able-Bodied Gaze)

Itwatches   *alwayswatches*
It walks behind me in the park and proceeds
to walk slowly to get a good look   *It*
follows&follows&follows   *&watches&watches*
&watches   I turn around   and

Itlooksaway   I begin to walk as
quickly as I can   gaining some speed but
Itfindsme I stop. *Itstops* I walk slowly again
Itwalksslowlybehindmeagain   Finally I
turn around to say: HELLO   but
Itpretends I'm   inconsequential that I   am
being paranoid   *It* was just minding its own
business all along

       Why am I bothering *It?*
    My mistake

          Itlooks up at the sun feeling absolved
Ityawns   *It's bored* of me already

DAVID WHEATLEY

Dyspraxia Ode

can you   can you
locate   in a crowded field   locate
        the one thing   necessary

amid the huge   redundancies   of violent effort
        do objects spin   from your grasp
when the drawn   string of   possibility
                tenses   snaps

        did you experience   difficulties
        finding your way here   do you sometimes find
the everyday   impossible

                experience   a falling short
        in   through   but for which
                the parts of speech   turn like

        wards of a key   in the wrong lock

        these are   my findings

        the lavish kindnesses   of incapacity
humoured   fret in the shadow   of a shame

        persistence that leaky tug   sails on a shambles
                wheezing sedition   and the swells beyond
the frosted portholes   follow no trade route

        set course for   no harbour
the jumping horizon   and your seasickness   are one

        howbeit now and then   in the piled wave's shadow
a need is felt   to trace   the pattern
        in the sweat of   a blindness

            to enter   the mouth
        of the unspeaking   and know its name

JEAN 'BINTA' BREEZE

riddym ravings

(the mad woman's poem)

de fus time dem kar me go a Bellevue
was fit di dactar an de lan lord operate
an tek de radio outa mi head
troo dem seize de bed
weh did a gi mi cancer
an mek mi talk to nobady
ah di same night wen dem trow mi out fi no pay de rent
mi haffi sleep outa door wid de Channel One riddym box
an de D.J. fly up eena mi head
mi hear im a play seh

Eh, Eh,
no feel no way
town is a place dat ah really kean stay
dem kudda – ribbit mi han
eh – ribbit mi toe
mi waan go a country go look mango

fah wen hungry mek King St pavement
bubble an dally in front a mi yeye
an mi foot start wanda falla fly
to de garbage pan eena de chinaman backlat
dem nearly chap aff mi han eena de butcha snap
fi de piece a ratten poke
ah de same time de mawga gal in front a mi
drap de laas piece a ripe banana
an mi – ben dung – pick i up – an nyam i
a dat time dem grab mi an kar mi back a Bellevue
dis time de dactar an de lanlord operate

an tek de radio plug outa mi head
den sen mi out, seh mi alright
but – as ah ketch back outa street
ah push een back de plug
an ah hear mi D.J. still a play, seh

Eh, Eh,
no feel no way
town is a place dat ah really kean stay
dem kudda – ribbit mi han
eh – ribbit mi toe
mi waan go a country go look mango

Ha Haah… Haa

wen mi fus come a town
mi use to tell everybady 'mawnin'
but as de likkle rosiness gawn outa mi face
nobady nah ansa mi
silence tun rags roun mi bady
in de mids a all de dead people dem
a bawl bout de caast of livin
an a ongle one ting tap mi tram go stark raving mad
a wen mi siddung eena Parade
a tear up newspaper fi talk to
sometime dem roll up
an tun eena one a Uncle But sweet saaf
yellow heart breadfruit
wid piece a roas saalfish side a i
an if likkle rain jus fall
mi get cocanat rundung fi eat i wid
same place side a weh de country bus dem pull out
an sometime mi a try board de bus
an de canductor bwoy a halla out seh

'dutty gal, kum affa de bus'
ah troo im no hear de riddym eena mi head
same as de tape weh de bus driva a play, seh

Eh, Eh,
no feel no way
town is a place dat ah really kean stay
dem kudda – ribbit mi han
eh – ribbit mi toe
mi waan go a country go look mango
so country bus, ah beg yuh
tek mi home
to de place, where I belang

an di dutty bway jus run mi aff

Well, dis mawnin, mi start out pon Spanish Town Road,
fah mi deh go walk go home a country
fah my granny use to tell mi how she walk tram wes
come a town
come sell food
an mi waan ketch home befo dem put de price pon i'
but mi kean go home dutty?
fah mi parents dem did sen mi out clean
Ah!
see wan stanpipe deh!
so mi strip aff all de crocus bag dem
an scrub unda mi armpit
fah mi hear de two mawga gal dem laas nite
a laugh an seh
who kudda breed smaddy like me?
a troo dem no-know seh a pure nice man
weh drive car an have gun
visit my piazza all dem four o'clock a mawnin

no de likkle dutty bwoy dem weh mi see dem a go home wid
but as mi feel de clear water pon mi bady
no grab dem grab mi
an is back eena Bellevue dem kar mi
seh mi mad an a bade naked a street
well dis time de dactar an de lanlord operate
an dem tek de whole radio tram outa mi head
but wen dem tink seh mi unda chloroform
dem put i dung careless
an wen dem gawn
mi tek de radio
an mi push i up eena mi belly
fi keep de baby company
fah even if mi nuh mek i
me waan my baby know dis yah riddym yah
tram before she bawn
hear de D.J. a play, seh

Eh, Eh,
no feel no way
town is a place dat ah really kean stay
dem kudda – ribbit mi han
eh – ribbit mi toe
mi waan go a country go look mango

an same time
de dactar an de lanlord
trigger de electric shack
an mi hear de D.J. vice bawl out, seh

Murther
Pull up Missa Operator!

V

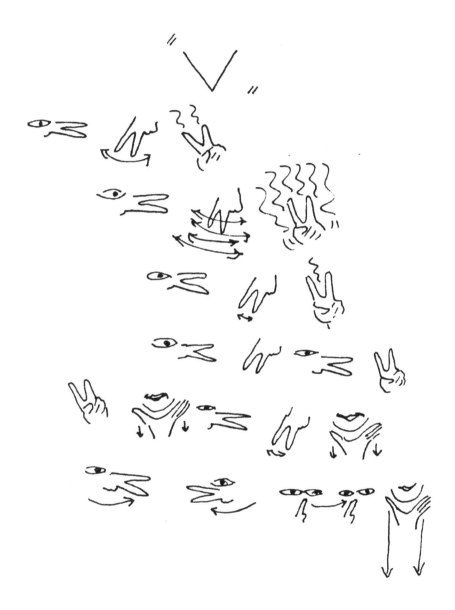

LEVENT BEŞKARDEŞ

V

I see you dancevibrate before me
And I vergevacillate the pen that pivotjots on the blank paper
I see you danceblur in accelerated velocity
And I jolt the pen that quickly veervaults vaultveers

I see you waltz langvalourously
Come and go velvetvolleying on the paper
I see you Venus vanishdance
On my vividview paper of vitality

You give me your beauty life to life
Volantwave of our meeting of minds

Link to original poem: https://www.youtube.com/watch?v=yOGzP2RcCNE
translated from French Sign Language by Stephanie Papa

PETRA KUPPERS

Craniosacral Rhythms

Earthquakes everywhere my head
hurts till she touches.
Her hand on my forehead.
Her hand on my breastbone.
Blood magma and lymph touch plates
send them shiver,
suspend in skin sacks
the corrugated surface of the cortex.

Fissures and sulci: larger and smaller divisions,
huge surfaces wrapped inward. Our memories fold
around each others' fingers. Let me kiss the spot

where the electrodes fastened to her temples
reset neurons, Frankensteinian fire
old techniques of fluids, electricity, and storms.

Continents beneath, iceberg depth
into the brainstem, reptilian ur-mama flaps her tail,
search for connection. Japan may fold,
California inch further away from Nevada:
we rest here, our plates in thrall with each other,
ping our way into our skulls, cover, cover,
till the borders break open cannot release

member post-traumatic recursions
member vulnerable stories
we burn white bright.

SHAHD ALSHAMMARI

Injections

As the needle pierces through your soft skin, you flinch
in reaction. You were always afraid
of needles, afraid of the sight of blood.
But without the medication, there is no hope,
and without the stabbing, there is no healing.
If I could fill all of my syringes with you
I would inject myself five times a day
and make you my routine, part of my daily prayers.
You are a drug I hope nobody else discovers.

DEAN ATTA

Five Litres of Blue

I used to think the blood in this body
was five litres of blue,
that only when I bled was it red.

I looked it up and found out
the blue of our veins is a trick of the light.
Human blood is always red,
sometimes crimson, sometimes bright.

Where do blue feelings come from?
I could be at the table with family: blue.
In a nightclub with friends: blue.
In the arms of a lover: blue.

Writing this poem for you: I used to
think of writing as some kind of bleeding.
That colour people stop and notice,
red of accidents, homicide or self-harm.

I used to think the blood in this body
was five litres of blue. How else
could I explain blue feelings to you?

ONA GRITZ

No

The nurses shaped us into positions.
Cradle hold, football hold. My hands
couldn't take you to the right place.
Cerebral palsy I mumbled, apology,
explanation. As though those experts
of the body didn't already know.
Finally, they propped cushions around us.
Your lips touched my breast
but instead of suckling, you dozed.
This had the nurses worried.
I worried how I'd feed you alone.
That night, your wail woke me.
I scooped you up, found the nurse's bell.
When a new one came, I shyly
explained the pillows, the palsy.
'No,' she said coolly and I stared.
'No. That baby needs sleep not milk.'
I tried again: 'he's hungry.'
Shaking her head, she left our room.
I attempted the football hold.
The cradle. Tried setting up pillows
then sitting between them. They fell.
Keeping you in my arms, I paced, I sang.
We cried in unison, both of us
so helpless, so desperately new.

NUALA WATT

Disabled Person's Travel Card

Council, council, let me on the bus
That you let me on last week.
Oh no Ms Watt, you can't go on the bus
For we don't know where you live.
So off I went to get proof of address
And I thought I'd sorted out the mess
But the council tore it up.

Council, council let me on the bus
That you let me on last week.
Oh no, Ms Watt, you can't go on the bus
For we need a doctor's note.
So I got them a note to make it clear
That I'm still disabled, like last year.
But the council tore it up.

Council, council, let me on the bus
That you let me on last week.
Oh no Ms Watt, you can't go on the bus.
We need two sick notes, not one.
The neurologist said 'I know you know
That cerebral palsy won't just go.
Still, here's a form to tell them so.'
But the council tore it up.

Council, council, let me on the bus
With my lifelong reasons why.
Oh no Ms Watt, you can't go on the bus
For your picture isn't straight.

So I sent a note to my MSP
And he wrote a poem in praise of me.
But the council tore it up.

Council, council, let me on the bus
With my lifelong reasons why.
Oh no Ms Watt, you can't go on the bus
For you're trying to rip us off.
I showed the form to my sister-in-law
And we typed all night till our nerves were raw
But the council tore it up.

Council, council, let me on the bus
With my pile of paperwork.
Oh no, Ms Watt, you can't go on the bus.
We require a note from God.
So I went to church and knelt to pray.
God sent me a letter the very next day.
But the council tore it up.

Council, council, stop. I've had enough.
I've had all that I can stand.
Oh good. Your application went
Exactly as we planned.

MISHKA HOOSEN

What wasn't said to the doctor

(for my family, whose light guided me home)

Doctor, things are starting to escape me,
and they'll keep at it you say,
keep running till they're gone,
or washed to blurring, so many words carved and lost
on this ragged slate you map
on scans, point out
patiently. I can control this, stop it with these,
you say. As long as you take them,
it'll curb things.

I'm not afraid of dying, and tonight
I'm going to take a long drag of smoke
and sleep alone. Content
as someone far from any kind of home may be
content, when things follow the course expected.
We take our small comforts this way: maps
and dosages, meds and morning faints,
your voice running over everything
like a loudspeaker, announcing,
interrupting the talking, the loving, the hundred
ungovernable impulses and words, that stupid attempt
at the fence. The night is a front
and my hands are burned.
Tonight I'm going to stretch out on the bed
like a riverbank in moonlight, like a snowbank
in March. Such quiet furies, the rough bones rising
triumphant from the grass.

Sleep easy by your wife
tonight. I mean this with tenderness,
Doctor: it's all I know
how to do, with these my nineteen years
half-caged. Hold
the throat of things, let the blood ring under the skin
in love or violence. Come to know the world
on the edge of a blade singing
with its striving. Take this small quarter
from a tired enemy.

I have never felt the cold
so keenly. My legs
fail me. My hands are too weak
to hold this pen. My name
is a memory
on that rain-marred slate.
But here is the knife-edge I will win it from.
This has hollowed my bones
for flight. Bring them all in, sign
the charts, call it
a difficult night. There's the vial on the shelf,
and my arm so bare
and waiting.

Madwomen have a propensity
for arson, or drowning. Leave nothing
unattended. I am that howl
in the night ward. I am electric
without your help. Rampant. I sing
the nursery songs. It's as they said. Fill the veins
with whatever you've got. Your small life
is beating itself white with fear
as laboratory rats in the half-light. White as the bed,
blank with fear as the bed.

KATE DAVIS
Hand-writing practice

When the boy saw it, his mouth went from *Smile* to *Watching Frankenstein*. The words he didn't say said *Cripple*, said *Pity*. The people with her stopped dead and listened and the small warm evening stopped dead and listened. It was *Pity* that stayed on his face as he offered her a suspended sentence – the chance to run and hide it before his friend who'd asked her if she fancied going to the Roxy on Saturday night got there and saw it too. And she was going to be grateful for his kindness. But then she wasn't. When they'd gone she picked up a chip of limestone, scratched a couple of letters in the dirt.

KERRY HARDIE

Flesh

Sitting in a doorway,
in October sunlight,
eating
peppers, onions, tomatoes,
stale bread sodden with olive oil –

and the air high and clean,
and the red taste of tomatoes,
and the sharp bite of onions,
and the pepper's scarlet crunch –

the body
coming awake again,
thinking,
maybe there's more to life than sickness,
than the body's craving for oblivion,
than the hunger of the spirit to be gone –

and maybe the body belongs in the world,
maybe it knows a thing or two,
maybe it's even possible
it may once more remember

sweetness,
absence of pain.

LUCIA PERILLO

Shrike Tree

Most days back then I would walk by the shrike tree,
a dead hawthorn at the base of a hill.
The shrike had pinned smaller birds on the tree's black thorns
and the sun had stripped them of their feathers.

Some of the dead ones hung at eye level
while some burned holes in the sky overhead.
At least it is honest,
the body apparent
and not rotting in the dirt.

And I, having never seen the shrike at work,
can only imagine how the breasts were driven into the branches.
When I saw him he'd be watching from a different tree
with his mask like Zorro
and the gray cape of his wings.

At first glance he could have been a mockingbird or a jay
if you didn't take note of how his beak was hooked.
If you didn't know the ruthlessness of what he did –
ah, but that is a human judgment.

They are mute, of course, a silence at the center of a bigger silence,
these rawhide ornaments, their bald skulls showing.
And notice how I've slipped into the present tense
as if they were still with me.

Of course they are still with me.

They hang there, desiccating
by the trail where I walked, back when I could walk,
before life pinned me on its thorn.
It is ferocious, life, but it must eat
then leaves us with the artifact.

Which is: these black silhouettes in the midday sun
strict and jagged, like an Asian script.
A tragedy that is not without its glamour.
Not without the runes of the wizened meat.

Because imagine the luck! – to be plucked from the air,
to be drenched and dried in the sun's bright voltage –
well, hard luck is luck, nonetheless.
With a chunk of sky in each eye socket.
And the pierced heart strung up like a pearl.

STEPHANIE HEIT

[Written on the inside of the napkin accompanying the dinner trays for psych unit patients admitted for ECT treatment. Located in the inpatient discharge folder thanks to a mental health worker double agent working for ETC. THE RESISTANCE. Placed behind the safety plan worksheet that is not safe.]

READ THIS IN PRIVATE. SHARE WITH OTHER INMATES CAREFUL TO NOT ALERT THE KEEPERS OR THE SHOCK BRIGADE

If you are receiving this note, you are in dire circumstances. Last ditch effort, any measures to keep you here. No doubt the 'treatment' you are scheduled for has been touted as extremely effective with unbelievable success rates. They are unbelievable for a reason. Perhaps you watched the propaganda video with the soft colors & spa-like ambience – more luxury vacation than let's shoot kilowatts through your brain & hope for the best. No doubt they reassured you the memory loss is just around the time of treatment; the side effect of long term memory loss flashed on the screen for less than a second & not spoken out loud. You are told this is your best bet. Your loved ones, at a loss for what to do, jump on board because the ones with the white coats & MD by their names know best.

RUN. Get up out of the gurney & get the hell out. NOW. Slip your wristband off & make like a normate out of there. You may be like I was – indifferent, deathwish-ridden, an easy consent signature. Take my word. Take my body. Better, take my mind as amnesiac evidence. LEAVE. Tell them you ate food, which will buy you time. Retract your consent. If you are involuntary or a minor, we are coming to get you. At the bottom of this page is a contact. We are waiting for you. We are a tuned network nimble to alternative options, focused on thrive rather than survive, resourced & ready to receive you.

ETC. THE RESISTANCE

TORRIN A. GREATHOUSE

Essay Fragment: Medical Model of Disability

The ~~disabled~~ body is always closest   to machine

in its dysfunction.   Most fixable

when it is furthest from human   body

as metaphor/rhetorical question:

If a clock is broken   do you repair it   or

ask the world to conform   to its sense of time.[1]

~~Disabled~~ body as abnormality.   Outlier

that must be removed   from the data

for more *accurate* results.   Medical Model[2]   speaks

says people [with disabilities] need to work   harder

to overcome [themselves].   The cure is to make them

more normal.[3]   my ~~disabled~~ body is a price tag

is scalpel bait   a prayer to hospital ceilings

or my ~~disabled~~ body is a weight on society.[4]

The Medical Model says: my ~~disabled~~ body

is like any disease.   If we discover a new & hungry

sickness   is it our duty to cure it   or to let it be?

---

[1] You must fix what is holding you back.

[2] Formally *Functional-Limitation Model*; formally *Biological-Inferiority Model*.

[3] Read: less disabled.

[4] Another price tag.

MADAILÍN BURNHOPE

Camel Girl

I am called the camel girl for my knees bend backwards.
I am called the camel girl for my back makes a mountain
from a molehill, except mobile, so saddle me up
with a tiny child; see me carry them.
I am called the camel girl for when I was named
it sounded kinder than table, tuffet or footstool girl.
I am called the camel girl for I kick like fuck when mad.
I am called the camel girl for my projectile drool.
I am called the camel girl for you wouldn't believe
how much water I can neck
back or shoulder to keep cool.
I am called the camel girl for I plan to go to school
and be introduced to the class on the basis
I've travelled in show business for four years
as a freight train, bread and butter, a skivvy,
was not, never will be, anyone's show-and-tell.
I am called the camel girl for I make
my dough on all fours
because it's easier, though I can stand up well,
so camel girl is an act, and it is not me
but the punters who are contractually compelled
to roll up every day, continuously, till they die.
I am Ella Harper, it is 1886, and I quit, for
I am fit for another occupation.

DANIEL SLUMAN

the beautiful

white sheets contain us in the illusion of containment
        & we don't screw like they do on tv

                the vaseline-smeared lens
         groping bodies that gleam

         the carefully-placed sighs
            & glazed eyes of the beautiful

     swimming through the windows of gyms
          & pools like torchlight

    lonely as hell
they will never love like this

     our whole bodies into the earth
        of each other

we bury ourselves like readers in books
    take each other apart

        & put each other back again & again

        cripples love best
      because love is an assembly

           & we have always been broken

        gluing our lives with glitter & card
         in darkened rooms

YU XIUHUA

A Leaky Boat

Secrets or origins untraced by history
omit the trouble of lies through a snowstorm

For forty years, it's been coaxed back by a larger wave to the shallow area
It plays with fish and shrimp
A gifted wind hunter that catches wind language, a snake in a cup

The boat has just endured two voids
One leaks out its body into a starry sky in the lake
Another leaks into the fish in its body

Starry night, again a starry night, the fish are nowhere
A fish doesn't know a man has come
and left traces in the boat

This is the only boat that confesses to being a boat
on a desolate shore
the nature of wood from a past life, and water of this time

translated from the Chinese by Fiona Sze-Lorrain

CYNTHIA HUNTINGTON

The Rapture

I remember standing in the kitchen, stirring bones for soup,
and in that moment, I became another person.

It was an early spring evening, the air California mild.
Outside, the eucalyptus was bowing compulsively

over the neighbor's motor home parked in the driveway.
The street was quiet for once, and all the windows were open.

Then my right arm tingled, a flutter started under the skin.
Fire charged down the nerve of my leg; my scalp exploded

in pricks of light. I shuddered and felt like laughing;
it was exhilarating as an earthquake. A city on fire

after an earthquake. Then I trembled and my legs shook,
and every muscle gripped so I fell and lay on my side,

a bolt driven down my skull into my spine. My legs were
swimming against the linoleum, and I looked up at the underside

of the stove, the dirty places where the sponge didn't reach.
Everything collapsed there in one place, one flash of time.

There in my body. In the kitchen at six in the evening. April.
A wooden spoon clutched in my hand, the smell of chicken broth.

And in that moment I knew everything that would come after:
the vision was complete as it seized me. Without diagnosis,

without history, I knew that my life was changed.
I seemed to have become entirely myself in that instant.

Not the tests, examinations in specialists' offices, not
the laboratory procedures: MRI, lumbar puncture, electrodes

pasted to my scalp, the needle scraped along the sole of my foot,
following one finger with the eyes, EEG, CAT scan, myelogram.

Not the falling down or the blindness and tremors, the stumble
and hiss in the blood, not the lying in bed in the afternoons.

Not phenobarbitol, amitriptylene, prednisone, amantadine, ACTH,
cortisone, cytoxan, copolymer, baclofen, tegretol, but this:

Six o'clock in the evening in April, stirring bones for soup.
An event whose knowledge arrived whole, its meaning taking years

to open, to seem a destiny. It lasted thirty seconds, no more.
Then my muscles unlocked, the surge and shaking left my body

and I lay still beneath the white high ceiling. Then I got up
and stood there, quiet, alone, just beginning to be afraid.

JAMIE HALE

Fibrotic

Fibrosis *n*: the thickening and scarring of connective
tissue usually after an injury

If you graft orange buds onto a lemon tree,
they grow together – a salad tree of
sharpness and sugar – or the bud dies.
Connecting two incompatible things is
harder than you would think – the body
knows this; the trees told me the same.
Maybe while I slept, a tree was grafted
onto me. My rootstock rots; Necrotic
buds flower from my heel. Sometimes
lightening splits a tree hollow like a
cave, but it still grows spindly branches.
Nobody told it it was broken or maybe it
always knew. Both are possible – hollow
things grow strangely. And yet we grow.
Trauma changes our genetic sequence. I
am fibrosed. My muscles become
woody. Trees grow thicker year on year.
I thin. But I have roots. My legs are trees,
leech nutrients? No. Drain poison. The
puckering sharpness of crabapple before
it's boiled with endless sugar. Sour fruit
brings a longer harvest, grafted to an
apple tree, but do not try to eat them
whole. The cold splinters my branches,
cracks appear in my skin. I swapped
transient legs for permanent bark. A tree
doesn't travel. It doesn't need to; it knows

the forest, sends signals beneath the floor. Swaps breadth for depth. Trees whisper at night. People don't notice. I've been blessed with ears that hear voices that others don't. Or do they miss voices that others hear? The grafted tree is neither one nor another; nor is it both. Maybe I just dreamed I was a tree. But I store carbon dioxide at night. Or I did.

The machine breathes for me now.

GWYNETH LEWIS

Will I?

The herb called Will I Ever Feel
Better? is to be used
only to treat the gravest wounds

that must – despite the patient's protests –
be kept open, so they can heal
from the inside out. Summer comes, summer

goes. So little recovery. Being alive
is both trauma and sovereign
remedy. You cannot choose.

IYANUOLUWA ADENLE

Beneath the Waves

I am not terrified
of the dark. I do not know
if the arms of God
would hold me
like poetry has done
every time my floater resurfaces
as I spiral beneath the waves.

When I break, does God break too?
Why must I do all the breaking alone?
Look at all the healing
this body has had to betray
breaking itself over and over.

ADRIENNE LEDDY

Erupture

My body
    cracks,
        splits,
            ruptures,

A bleeding daily rebirth.

My land is my body is carved out from seismic churning
And a deep, aching pain
Echoing over millennia.

Ripping itself open and gives way to:
Nothing.

Our creation from darkness, life through death,
Molded from red earth and saltwater
And a deeply aching grief which gave us our first breaths.

My strong people hardened by clay
And born to withstand the centuries.

So –

While I lay here broken and shattered,
My pieces laid out on my bed,
Carefully wetting my shards of clay to get back to something I can
   recognise,
I ask myself:

Did Fu'una mold me wrong?

Is it a mistake that leaves my red earth cracking, splitting, rupturing?

Am I still split like our mountains,
           do I need a millennia more to form beautiful?

These questions when I'm once again decaying alone with a heating pad
Like amot of ancestors' hot oil massaged in skin
Unknowingly sculpting my own urban tradition…
And I remember.

No, this can't be a mistake…

This pain can raise mountains and draw rainbows in the sky.

This lonely island, one I'm sure I'll die on,
Lies surrounded by my relatives in the ocean of our ancestors.

And this insurmountable grief is a wave that breathes life back to me.

Our creation story is of the siblings Puntan and Fu'una whose lives were sacrificed to create life. Through their loss came all of us as Chamorro people, and in processing the harsh reality of chronic pain I find comfort in relating my own journey to our creation story, and a renewed love for my body despite the pain it can bring me.

RACHAEL JOHNSON

You Tear Out My Tongue

and hang it on the line / It shudders
in the dull Albuquerque breeze and cracks
like a whip with each dry

gust / Fat bees jerk
back and forth before they settle
to scrape their limbs

against its wet husk / I watch pale
day-moths flicker
close to sip the draining

nectar / Finally,
it becomes a bloodless
thing, curling like a scream
in the heat –

LEROY F. MOORE JR

Disabled World Nation

War, torture, poverty, pollution
Increasing disabled population
No rehabilitation, no medication, no education
the poorest of the poor
Government doesn't need you any more
war-torn countries
creates lack of mobility
Limbs blown to pieces
can't miss a non-moving target
Don't you get it
we're becoming a Disabled World Nation
Police brutality & government sanctions
are the womb of this creation
Got raped & impregnated with greed & corruption
passed down policies & charities
so liberals can make money
off disability and poverty
The majority of Disabled World Nation
are in third world countries
where disabled children die before they're twenty
Millions are starving
in war and peace time
While the United Nations
celebrate Disability Awareness
many become disabled cause of UN's lack of action
Missiles & chemical warfare
no health care or welfare
the only occupation is begging
Forced to rely on your enemies
to bring economic stability

Foreign laws, theories & therapy
invading third world countries

The Disabled World Nation
has the numbers
but lacks the political & economic power
Different country but same story
Walking on landmines
war disables the body, soul, and mind
No vaccine for common illness
police shooting people with mental illness
all die because of a lack of humanity
Children playing in the rubble
stepping on their parents' dead bodies
have to deal with war, poverty, & disability with no family
Developed & underdeveloped countries have many things in common
under the Disabled World Nation
Institutionalising, segregation, malnutrition
misrepresentation & pity
molded, formed & displayed by the media
Gifts and donations
don't trickle down to the needy
We aren't even in control in our own organisations
Who will break this cycle
Nothing About Us Without Us
a slogan held up high by disabled South Africans
but their voices are buried by day-to-day struggles
Who will take a stand against war
on a disabled platform
Radicals and revolutionaries go against the norm
leaders of the Disabled World Nation are lukewarm
Scattering for food droppings
the Disabled World Nation
treated worse than animals

exploiting their disabilities so they can eat

crawling on their hands and knees

cause technology is not even a dream

Living on a different type of plantation

in which the government, sometimes your parents,

and yes, our own organisations are the Masters

I can go on but this is getting depressing

it's time to stop the growth of the Disabled World Nation

War fuels the Disabled World Nation

ILYA KAMINSKY

That Map of Bone and Opened Valves

I watched the Sergeant aim, the deaf boy take iron and fire in his mouth –
his face on the asphalt,
that map of bones and opened valves.
It's the air. Something in the air wants us too much.
The earth is still.
The tower guards eat cucumber sandwiches.
This first day
soldiers examine the ears of bartenders, accountants, soldiers –
the wicked things silence does to soldiers.
They tear Gora's wife from her bed like a door off a bus.
Observe this moment
– how it convulses –
The body of the boy lies on the asphalt like a paperclip.
The body of the boy lies on the asphalt
like the body of a boy.
I touch the walls, feel the pulse of the house, and I
stare up wordless and do not know why I am alive.
We tiptoe this city,
Sonya and I,
between theaters and gardens and wrought-iron gates –
Be courageous, we say, but no one
is courageous, as a sound we do not hear
lifts the birds off the water.

ABDULLAH AL-BARADOUNI

Why I Am Silent about the Lament

They tell me my silence is about lamentation.
I tell them the howling is ugly.

Poetry is only for life and I
felt like singing, not howling.

How do I call the dead now that between us are hushed
dirt and grave? I am surrounded by mute soil and a mausoleum.

Howling is only for widows and I am not
like a widow who wails on the silent casket.

translated from the Arabic by Threa Almontaser

G.N. SAIBABA

A Sparrow in My Cell

A sparrow
flew like an arrow
into my cell
through the bars
on a chilling desolate
midnight.

He perched
on the parapet wall
of the toilet
with little jumps
waveringly.

I tried to whisper
deliriously something to the bird
through my half-closed,
sleepy and hallucinating eyes.

A fat officer giggled
with his rocky grim face
hurrying through
his midnight rounds
behind a bony guard.

My gaze flew back
to the little creature
in my waking dream.

Trying to fly out,
he narrowly hit a bar
and fell to the floor
with a sound of susurration
like the moaning of my numb heart.

A night train
whistled at a faraway station
like a ghost of a fallen civilisation.
Gaining consciousness and courage,
the bird walked around
the floor of my cell
pecking at tiny spots.

The guard returned
to the yard rubbing
his tired eyes of surveillance
taking long strides up and down.

The little bird
climbed on to my bed
and sat at my painful
and trembling feet.
I held my breath.
Slowly, he started walking
on the corners of my bed
moving his eyes
this way and that way
as if saying something to me
or measuring my heartbeats.

An owl outside
the high security walls
howled a horrible shriek.

Perhaps, the little one
lost his way,
or his nest
or his loved one,
I thought.

Suddenly,
he fluttered his wings
flying to the ceiling
and dashing down to the floor.
An ugly siren shrilled.
The guards changed their duties.
The lifeless night groaned once again.

I felt my throat parched;
but how could I take water
with the bird around in my cell?

Slipping back
into my distant dream,
I whispered to him:
My friend,
come every night
I am terribly lonely.

LES MURRAY

Dog Fox Field

> The test for feeblemindedness was, they had to make up
> a sentence using the words *dog*, *fox* and *field*.
>
> JUDGEMENT AT NUREMBERG

These were no leaders, but they were first
into the dark on Dog Fox Field:

Anna who rocked her head, and Paul
who grew big and yet giggled small,

Irma who looked Chinese, and Hans
who knew his world as a fox knows a field.

Hunted with needles, exposed, unfed,
this time in their thousands they bore sad cuts

for having gazed, and shuffled, and failed
to field the lore of prey and hound

they then had to thump and cry in the vans
that ran while stopped in Dog Fox Field.

Our sentries, whose holocaust does not end,
they show us when we cross into Dog Fox Field.

GAELE SOBOTT

Exuviae

/ɪgˈzjuːvɪiː,ɛgˈzjuːvɪiː/
the cast or sloughed skin of an animal, especially of an insect larva.

*Have you ever ever ever…*seen

        my body become the exoskeleton of a long-legged sailor
a locust a snake
    no muscle no bones no flavour

    did you see me slip into this world following seven hours of
        hard labour
  an embryonic minority a mutated remake
        my body become the exoskeleton of a short-legged sailor

have you ever seen the contours of my fingertips   stitched together by a
    deformed tailor
         who sang as she sewed me a tiny genetic keepsake
    no muscle no bones no flavour

    have you seen the likes of Darwin's half cousin who view me as
        a traitor
  to the betterment of humanity an unwanted mistake
        my body become the exoskeleton of a bow-legged sailor

have you seen my knock-kneed wife breathe medicine from her inhaler
and yell *people consent when the Hitlers of this world exterminate us*
  for fuck sake
        no muscle no bones no flavour

and have you ever ever seen me emerge from that darkness as soft and
    wispy as vapour
        like a nymph seven years underground have you seen me pulsate
          and shake
      my body become the exoskeleton of a one-legged sailor
                            no muscle no bones no flavour

Based on the clapping song 'Long-legged Sailor'.
Darwin's half cousin refers to Francis Galton, an early eugenicist.

ANITA ENDREZZE
Song-Maker

There is a drunk on Main Avenue, slumped
in front of the Union Gospel Mission.
He is dreaming of pintos the color of wine
and ice, and drums that speak the names
of wind. His hair hides his face,
but I think I know him.

Didn't he make songs people still sing
in their sleep?
Didn't coyotes beg him for new songs
to give to the moon?
Didn't he dance all night once and laugh
when the women suddenly turned
shy at dawn?
Didn't he make a song just for me,
one blessed by its being sung only once?

If he would lift his face
I could see his eyes, see
if he's singing now
a soul-dissolving song.
But he's all hunched over
and everyone walks around him.
He must still have strong magic
to be so invisible.

I remember him saying
Even grass has a song,
though only wind hears it.

MEGAN FERNANDES
Letter to a Young Poet

If you haven't taken the Amtrak in Florida, you haven't lived. At 2:00 a.m., seven months into the pandemic, I'm looking up where Seamus Heaney died. It was Blackrock Clinic overlooking the sea and I wonder, sometimes, what is my thing with the Irish, but if the white kids can go to India for an epiphany, maybe it's fine that I go to Ireland. Don't read Melanie Klein in a crisis. She's depressing and there are alternatives. Like Winnicott or a lobotomy. Flow is best understood through Islamic mysticism or Lil Wayne spitting without a rhyme book, post-2003. To want the same things as you age is not always a failure of growth. A good city will not parent you. Every poet has a love affair with a bridge. Mine is the Manhattan and she's a middle child. Or the Sea Link in Mumbai, her galactic tentacles whipping the starless sky. When I say *bridge*, what I mean is goddess. People need your ideas more than your showmanship. LA is ruining some of you. All analysis is revisionist. Yellow wildflowers are it. It's better to be illegible, sometimes. Then they can't govern you. It takes time to build an ethics. Go slow. Wellness is a myth and shame transforms no one. You can walk off most anything. Everyone should watch anime after a heartbreak. Sleep upward in a forest so the animal sees your gaze. I think about that missing plane sometimes and what it means to go unrecovered. Pay attention to what disgusts you. Some of the most interesting people have no legacy. Remember that green is your color and in doubt, read Brooks. In the end, your role is to attend to the things you like and ask for more of it: Bridges. Ideas. Destabilisation. Yellow tansy. Cities. The wild sea. And in the absence of recovery, some ritual. In the absence of love? Ritual. Understand that ritual is a kind of patience, an awaiting and waiting. Keep waiting, kitten. You will be surprised what you can come back from.

LISA KELLY

Blackbird and Beethoven

Blackbird, you are *the Beethoven of songbirds*
but when I hear this, the metaphor summons
his bust, and I can't recall your call.

How many musicians, blackbird, are deaf
like the percussionist who taught herself to hear
with parts of her body other than her ears,

who performs barefoot to feel the music better?
If I'd known more about vibrations, blackbird,
how we hear with our hands with special nerve cells,

known that hearing, blackbird, is an audio-tactile experience,
with both senses tuned to environmental oscillations,
I could have countered his anecdote, the conductor

who claimed the percussionist was fake because she looked
round when he entered her dressing room. Blackbird, I
would have sung out your *chink chink* warning call.

When I see you in the ivy, blackbird,
I think of the thirteen ways of looking at you
and how you are a sign as well as a song.

Blackbird, you came before and after Beethoven,
you shaped phrases and motifs recorded
in his pocket notebook. You sing the opening

to the rondo of his violin concerto. I see him, blackbird,
as his housekeeper saw him – pencil in mouth,
a yellow beak, touching the other end to the soundboard

of a piano to feel the vibration of your song. Blackbird,
as he hits the notes harder, as the piano starts
to fall apart, will the fake musicians turn round?

JOANNE LIMBURG

The Alice Case

'The problem with Alice,' the Caterpillar says,
      'is her rigidity of thought.'

'Yes,' says Humpty Dumpty,
      'and her lack of empathy.'

'Indeed,' says the Caterpillar,
      'her mind-blindness.'

'Yes,' says Humpty Dumpty,
      'her inability to read faces.'

'Indeed,' says the Caterpillar,
      'or tone of voice.'

'And then,' says Humpty Dumpty,
      'there's the flatness of her affect.'

'Alongside,' says the Caterpillar,
      'the strangeness of her prosody…'

'…as well as,' says Humpty Dumpty,
      'her adherence to routine.'

'Not forgetting,' says the Caterpillar,
      'her repetitive behaviours.'

'Or her failure,' says Humpty Dumpty,
      'to understand a joke.'

'Or her lack,' says the Caterpillar,
     'of any feel for metaphor.'

'Or her inability,' says Humpty Dumpty,
     'to hold a proper conversation…'

'Excuse me,' says Alice.
     'May I say something?'

'Of course,' says the Caterpillar,
     'you may say something –'

'Yes,' says Humpty Dumpty,
     'and we'll tell you why it's wrong.'

FRANK ORMSBY

Once a Day

I take my hallucinations for a walk
once a day at the Waterworks, that is to say
I assume they accompany me.
Acres of fresh air, some trees, a lake –
plenty of space to practise disappearing.
Would the dogs detect an aura or take a snarl
at the invisible? I expected not.

I expected right. Park life has its own concerns.
The heron gathers North around him
like a monk's habit and appears to sleep.
The 'Joggers Against Oblivion' are already
on a gasping break. Only the terrier,
Stupid Fucker, draws near and growls, then
turns to the more urgent business of his life,
chasing a ball for the angriest man in Ireland.

ZUO YOU

Bluff

People
are
often
close to my ear,
covering their mouth
and telling me
loudly
something trivial.

translated from the Chinese by Yi Zhe

BRANDI BIRD

Ode to Diabetes

God answered my prayers. Pray for sickness,
not illness. Pray to be rouge-cheeked, prayer for sweat.

Let my pancreas die. The all + flesh, pinprick of a glucometer
on my finger, trigger rosary bead, smudged insulin in my stomach fat,

medicinal clouds. A sky darkened by endocrine storms, metabolic
shock, the awe of sweat & rain. Sweet smell of piss, a perfume

called abundance worn in church when I was eleven years old in a white
dress. Pneumonia when I was twelve, my father in the oxygen

tank, breathing him, incense & rawhide. When I got better I ate
attention, praise for being alive. There is no praise now. A needle,

a sharps box, yellow asking me to slow down. I eat an apple & it spikes
my glucose. Dawn phenomena, the sun phenomena, a phenomenon

of language & its failures in the light of day. Gibiskwad,
mixed gland in the anishinaabemowin medical dictionary. There is an error

in the way I speak, the way I eat. My mouth is inhuman. It curls
when I'm punished. Prayer for when I'm better, when I better

take care of myself. Prayer for hiding insulin from my father. Prayer
for the ritual at bedtime, the grip on the needle, the punc-

ture, the pump. There is no pill to dry-swallow now.
Medicine is subcutaneous. It's molten & changes form.

Insulin collects in pools like holy water I'd sneak sips of in church.
All those babies baptised in basins I put my lips on. Let God

run through me like sugar. Like He's so sweet, I'll gag.

I.S. JONES

Self-Portrait as the Blk Girl Becoming the Beast Everyone Thought She Was

the moon is my first emotion   then beast   then happy rage
   depending on a zealous appetite

i pull bobby pins   from the kitchen of my scalp   tear out nails

one by one   pluck out the lashes   yank docile teeth

        fold the skin back by the mouth   i release my human flesh
           & night drops

   blue wolves circle the block in acute madness
dreaming in gun smoke & new names to pick their fangs clean

         the moon sways blood & voices behind yellow eyes
         each of the names bows inside me

i grin   & the moon is an anxious pulse   i   a hungry one

        in overexposure   the moon could make anything feral
   i only eat a macabre light   & the night is so sweet on my tongue

   fear makes the blue wolves multiply
the moon rummages through the light of my name like a vagrant beggar

    tills the blood in my four-legged body

        born non-white & woman   call the thing what it is:

hostile   uppity   neck-rolls   hips without the logic   mean
    mugs   vengeful at the root

    but you've only known   my mercy

a snatched tongue: polite hands: crossed legs: a settled throat: plea &
    please two hands on the same body

                never my unhinged joy

in my first language – the cease of blood before writhing –

knuckling of bone & sinew   a blue neck caught inside a maw

& how each muscle negotiates   before severing

god of the faithful night   teach me to lose my mouth in reverie

    to laugh in my predator's blood   to let it fill my belly

how it trickles   through the floorboard of my teeth

SELIMA HILL

Snouts

Because I find it hard decoding faces,
I recognise the doctors by their shoes:

I see the shiny shoes as pairs of snouts
peeping out like the snouts of weasels.

KARL KNIGHTS
A Field Guide to Stares

There's the curious stares,
often from parents or old ladies.
They want to know more,
but don't know how to ask.

The gawkers. They want to know
what's wrong with you.
You'll want to punch
these people.

The friend. You spy
the strap of a splint
as they walk. You stare.
They stare back. You both smile; nod.

The anxious. The temporarily abled,
my friend calls them. They see
a possible future,
scowl and turn away.

SALEEM HUE PENNY

Tinniō: translation of a sound poem

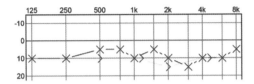

I ring,
like /____/ y'all
hear that /____/ right?

I^2,
I^2 jingle.
I^2,
I^2 clink.

It's like /____/ I
think? I pay,
t(o)o /____/ it seems,

I cry,
my ears → r ← eyes,
I scream, in a /____/ voice,
I plead,

To be, /____/ silently,
see the quieting,
be riling me,

Sighing or flying.
Gliding or diving.
Whispering, violently,
Drifting, *whiling...*ly.

I end before the end
begins & that
frēquish /____/ begins again,

This /____/
should be peace.
Yet, eye hear
/____/ beeps.

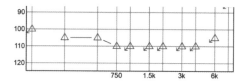

Experience the hybrid sound poem at
anothernewcalligraphy.com/shp-tinnio.html

KEI MILLER

The Subaltern Dreams of Big

> After brutally criticising the then Government's plan to build
> a new highway which would have profoundly upended the life
> of her community, a Trinidadian woman stood firm in her
> critique saying, 'Me eh fraid; I saying it in Big!'

Oh to say a thing in big – in monument,
in syllables more solid than statues;

       to say a thing not in drizzle or rain
but hurricane, in swell and surge,

the centre always still

but outside bands of wind lift
galvanised rooves like a sudden choir

giving back to the frenzied preacher,
his last words; oh,

to say a thing in drum, in what rumbles
across mountains and through canefields,

that trembles the wattled walls
of Quashie's shack: *behold,*

the day of the watchman
is coming; oh

to say a thing in obeah, in the broken
necks of white yard fowls, in the poured blood

of goats, in Sycorax, original
modder-woman walking cross the crest of hills,

pulling the moon till the night sea bubbles
up like a cauldron; oh

to say a thing plain, without if I may
            or should it please the court.
            or with all due respect;

to convene again, our parliaments,
to wear again, our crowns,

to recognise inside us what is dust
and bone and world and star; oh

to gather from our smallness,
that which is large –

GAYLE KENNEDY

After Viewing the Carved Trees Exhibition

Arborglyphs, Dendroglyphs
These are the scientific words
The white man uses to describe
Our tree writing, the sophisticated hieroglyphics
Of an ancient culture, an ancient civilisation
These are the words used to describe
The arboreal classrooms on which
Our ceremonies & laws were writ large
The sweat & blood of the carvers impregnating
The DNA of our people into the
Limbs of the sapwood and heartwood
That lined the pathway of learning
For the young warriors & their teachers

Did giving them these cold, hard words
Calling them the tree carvings of a primitive people,
Make it easier for the scientist,
The anthropologist, the land coveter
To rip them from their belonging place?
To destroy the warriors' classrooms or
Desecrate the graves of our lost ancestors?

Did they make it easier to rip
The memorial trees carved with
All the knowledge needed to
Provide a pathway for the
Spirit of the lost hero to
Find his way to the sky world?
Did they not see the rounded,
Almost fecund mound that was

The final resting place of someone
Whose loss caused such grief,
Much keening, wailing, & self inflicted
Physical pain to replace the deep
Agony of mourning?

Did those words blind them to the
Ancient knowledge contained
In the chevrons, the curvilinear, the scrolls?
Did they make them easy for people
To transplant them to their backyards
To stand beside the roses & grevilleas
And the transplanted weeds
Watered, & cut and tortured & tamed
Into green blankets to disguise the dust & earth
Of a land they could never really own?
Did they give them carte blanche
To place the trees in the dark, dank bowels of museums,
Those grand stone buildings, receivers of stolen goods
Repositories of not just ours
But other peoples' plundered cultures?

And our people, herded onto missions,
Their possum skin cloaks & kangaroo rugs
Replaced by burlap, hessian & calico
Their bush food by flour, sugar & tea and
Their spirits, their beliefs by the single god
Of the conquering peoples?
Did they dream of the Yammunyamun?
The impending initiation?
The invitations sent near & far
The feasting, the dancing, the singing?
Did they long for the comfort of their own ceremonies?
Their own way of being now gone and now

Replaced by the unfamiliar bought by
Ships, and bullock drays and horses?

And do we mob, the ancestors of
The carvers, the teachers, the initiated
Take comfort from the return of our trees
Or from the revelation of our lost
And forgotten ceremony
Or from the photos in black & white & faded sepia
Of a world and ways now gone?
Do we celebrate?
Do we own our anger
Or do we forgive?
Or do we let the tears
Fall where they may?

SHIKI ITSUMA

Loam

I work
the soil   it echoes with the footsteps of the world
I make my body tremble like a fallen leaf and sink
and I thirst for words of life which may bud in tomorrow's loam
Everyone seeks   from the sown seed
that by which green aromas   and harvest
plot cause and consequence into a single course
The sweat I sweat from this dabbling is lovely

Deaths by atom bomb   the chill touch of bones
blood dripping   the races and borders
of billions of people   Here we break them up
and compost sorrow

I
falteringly   with numb hands   work the soil beneath my feet
To these mud-clotted roots   which someday will lengthen in the dark
to this loam   the universal womb
all I do is listen

translated from the Japanese by John Newton Webb

AGHA SHAHID ALI

Not All, Only a Few Return

(after Ghalib)

Just a few return from dust, disguised as roses.
What hopes the earth forever covers, what faces?

I too could recall moonlit roofs, those nights of wine –
But Time has shelved them now in Memory's dimmed places.

She has left forever, let blood flow from my eyes
till my eyes are lamps lit for love's darkest places.

All is his – Sleep, Peace, Night – when on his arm your hair
shines to make him the god whom nothing effaces.

With wine, the palm's lines, believe me, rush to Life's stream –
Look, here's my hand, and here the red glass it raises.

See me! Beaten by sorrow, man is numbed to pain.
Grief has become the pain only pain erases.

World, should Ghalib keep weeping you will see a flood
drown your terraced cities, your marble palaces.

BADR SHĀKIR AL-SAYYĀB

Rain Song

Your eyes are two palm tree forests in early light,
Or two balconies from which the moonlight recedes
When they smile, your eyes, the vines put forth their leaves,
And lights dance…like moons in a river
Rippled by the blade of an oar at break of day;
As if stars were throbbing in the depths of them…
And they drown in a mist of sorrow translucent
Like the sea stroked by the hand of nightfall;
The warmth of winter is in it, the shudder of autumn,
And death and birth, darkness and light;
A sobbing flares up to tremble in my soul
And a savage elation embracing the sky,
Frenzy of a child frightened by the moon.
It is as if archways of mist drank the clouds
And drop by drop dissolved in the rain…
As if children snickered in the vineyard bowers,
The song of the rain
Rippled the silence of birds in the trees…
Drop, drop, the rain
Drip
Drop the rain

Evening yawned, from low clouds
Heavy tears are streaming still.
It is as if a child before sleep were rambling on
About his mother a year ago he went to wake her, did not find her,
Then was told, for he kept on asking,
'After tomorrow, she'll come back again'…
That she must come back again,
Yet his playmates whisper that she is there

151

In the hillside, sleeping her death for ever,
Eating the earth around her, drinking the rain;
As if a forlorn fisherman gathering nets
Cursed the waters and fate
And scattered a song at moonset,
Drip, drop, the rain
Drip, drop, the rain

Do you know what sorrow the rain can inspire?
Do you know how gutters weep when it pours down?
Do you know how lost a solitary person feels in the rain?
Endless, like spilt blood, like hungry people, like love,
Like children, like the dead, endless the rain.
Your two eyes take me wandering with the rain,
Lightnings from across the Gulf sweep the shores of Iraq
With stars and shells,
As if a dawn were about to break from them,
But night pulls over them a coverlet of blood.
I cry out to the Gulf: 'O Gulf,
Giver of pearls, shells and death!'
And the echo replies,
As if lamenting:
'O Gulf,
Giver of shells and death.'
I can almost hear Iraq husbanding the thunder,
Storing lightning in the mountains and plains,
So that if the seal were broken by men
The winds would leave in the valley not a trace of Thamud.
I can almost hear the palm trees drinking the rain,
Hear the villages moaning and emigrants
With oar and sail fighting the Gulf
Winds of storm and thunder, singing
'Rain…rain…
Drip, drop, the rain…'

And there is hunger in Iraq,
The harvest time scatters the grain in it,
That crows and locusts may gobble their fill,
Granaries and stones grind on and on,
Mills turn in the fields, with the men turning…
Drip, drop, the rain…
Drip
Drop
When came the night for leaving, how many tears we shed,
We made the rain a pretext, not wishing to be blamed
Drip, drop, the rain
Drip, drop, the rain
Since we had been children, the sky
Would be clouded in wintertime,
And down would pour the rain,
And every year when earth turned green the hunger struck us.
Not a year has passed without hunger in Iraq.
Rain…
Drip, drop, the rain…
Drip, drop…

In every drop of rain
A red or yellow color buds from the seeds of flowers.
Every tear wept by the hungry and naked people
And every spilt drop of slaves' blood
Is a smile aimed at a new dawn,
A nipple turning rosy in an infant's lips
In the young world of tomorrow, bringer of life.
Drip…
Drop…the rain… In the rain
Iraq will blossom one day
I cry out to the Gulf: 'O Gulf,
Giver of pearls, shells and death!'

The echo replies
As if lamenting:
'O Gulf,
Giver of shells and death.'
And across the sands from among its lavish gifts
The Gulf scatters fuming froth and shells
And the skeletons of miserable drowned emigrants
Who drank death forever
From the depths of the Gulf, from the ground of its silence,
And in Iraq a thousand serpents drink the nectar
From a flower the Euphrates has nourished with dew.
I hear the echo
Ringing in the Gulf:
'Rain...
Drip, drop, the rain...
Drip, drop.'

In every drop of rain
A red or yellow color buds from the seeds of flowers.
Every tear wept by the hungry and naked people
And every spilt drop of slaves' blood
Is a smile aimed at a new dawn,
A nipple turning rosy in an infant's lips
In the young world of tomorrow, bringer of life.
And still the rain pours down.

translated from the Arabic by Lena Jayyusi and Christopher Middleton

GOLAN HAJI

from **A Soldier in a Madhouse**

'Slow it!' when the raid came
and they gagged men with their leather belts,
my scream turned back in my throat
and wore away what was left of my language.
The numbness in my arm wakes up
too much I had lain myself on it
and I see all those who were staring at me just now
and the sutures of the air are unpicked as if they
      are my mouth and I hear nothing,
I stare at the dot in the dirty white
as it turns out to be an eye staring back at me,
and wherever I looked I found myself multiplying.
There are stares devouring me leave nothing but
               a crust
If I touch it with my fingertips I'd vanish.
I am the bread of the invisible:
how terrified I am by the eyes of the terrified,
everyone who's terrified, terrifies.

translated from the Arabic by Golan Haji and Stephen Watts

CYRÉE JARELLE JOHNSON

Now Let the Weeping Cease

after Jericho Brown
after Sophocles

On this land, the weeping time never ceased.
The river is safer than the shore.

The river is safer than the shore
and death is more than a shade who hums back.

My death is a shade that hums back at me.
My ghost hums back across time's night-vast gap.

Even the thought of a ghost bends time.
In which year is today situated?

Our situation is a spectral year,
a year dreamed as though it were a future.

A future soft as a child's daydreams.
My childhood daydreams did not feature me.

I could not picture a featured future.
Now I cast shadows with shades and the night.

CAT CHONG

—I accept the task from the sun—

—the moment of insight—circumstance of the spheres—I haven't
been able to tell you—right before the planets went mainstream—
from day 652 when the Singaporean government announced
it would allow vaccinated travellers from Canada—Denmark—
France—Italy—the Netherlands—Spain—the US and UK—we
think the same things at the same time—can't do anything about
it—after 650 days I'm granted approval from my institution to go
home—I don't care about the power of my passport out—an endless
as far as we nurture it—we can all make blood—the streetlights
never go out—the roots are a textured aura of anything fixed—
the loving will for contact—a difference in account—conditions
of degradation and dissolving ephemera—found in pledged
violence—is what these islands will do to you—my tongue is
feigning an abstraction—peering for lichen that I haven't seen
on public walkways or signposts in so many years—looking at a
parent's flat face on my phone screen—poetry inoculates me for the
shortest amount of time—I'm still moving in languages complicit
in ongoing genocide—remember this in every single tense—an
unlucky god or desperation—neither delusion—of my many
mothered tongue—there's a comma before the thunderstorm—
magnetism and irreparability—we put it on paper to discover it
outside ourselves—I don't want to keep it on the inside of my
mouth—or the new patient demographic intake form—I'll be right
back—these are my preferred proverbs—so tell me—medicine
asks—tell me who you are—

ANTHONY VAHNI CAPILDEO

Plague Poems

(for Jack Belloli)

I *Now We Are Things Invisible*

The inessential park is closed.
Its benches clean of homeless
bodies hurting less in sleep.
Cigs, wasteful pansies, gratuitous
marigolds, dogs running like flames
and vaguely sinister statues
are out, like fountains in drought.
The wrong romances will not fall
among its turning leaves. Who'd make
a fearful call, craving escape
from beatings, can't expect to coast
on help from public services.
The sky is roof only to birds
and drones, no place to lose the words
of crazymakers. You can grow
your inward silence indoors now
the inessential park is closed.
Memory restyles it like a scroll,
adding some willows, and a bridge
to which you run, to catch a wish.
The visible, unusable
park; its blue imagined bridge.
For love of things invisible.

II *Plague Fidelity*

You may kiss me as much as you
like. I wish you would. I always

wish you would. I wish you always
would. You're the only one allowed
to kiss me. The science is, lack
of touch can make you ill, even
physically. Sometimes when you
breathe, I start breathing just like you.
Do you remember grandmothers,
poems about grandmothers? You
said life's not like that. Could be.
Remember asking, laughing, why
I write – used to – about the sea?
Kiss me. Tell me where you are.

III *Coronavirus Swing*

What's different? Why is it different?
Why must we be, when we are not?
I'm beside myself. I'm with you.
For social dancing, read
social distancing. You alone do
I adore. For catastrophe
read charity. For adventure
read attentiveness. Oh baby,
I mean it.
      For mask, read ring.

IV *Flowers for the House*

There's a tiny lilac flower
with no name I ever could find,
in Trinidad. You'd notice it
at grass level, when you're a child.
If there are pandemic babies –
not like jail babies; they won't spring –
like workhouse babies – lives confined

after pregnancy's confinement –
what are the fairytales we need?
And how to explain about
going Outside? An enlarged heart
in a rocking chair dreams of games
it used to hide from, all the time
all the time also in the world.

V *Ecopoetic Pandemic Logic*

What's different? Why is it different?
Why must we be, when we are not?
People push for clear-cut heroes
and heroes' mirrors, enemies.
Who hears an alienating song
in an alienated land?
'We did not kill by bullets
as much as by chemicals
pouring softly into streams
far from cotton T-shirt malls.'
That won't work. Try this:
                              First they came
for the transport. Then they came for
the libraries, the hospitals,
the shelters, the helplines;
they came for your education.
Now they've come for our own good.
Do you agree? For our own good?

POLLY ATKIN

Breath Test

My breath got lost in the post. I sent
a box of it out, portioned in six
foil bags like space food rations. I addressed it
as instructed, sent it away, a long
exhale. Bated breath. It arrived

back at my door in the arms of the postman –
a large brown box of my breath – marked
addressee gone away. I held my breath
to my chest. My breath weighed next to nothing.

I had wasted my breath. It was a time
of crisis. I had to post my breath
to the hospital, to keep the hospital secure.
I could not go to the hospital and breathe.

I caught my breath. Six silver bags
like emergency blankets around my breath
mirrors to breathe on to check if you're living.
I took my breath away. My breath

returned to sender. It was not a love letter.
It was not a request. It was innovation.
I could not breathe at the hospital. It was
a time of crisis. It was a test.

I wanted to save my breath, but my breath
was out of me. I could not draw breath in
only let it go again, hoping
it held itself long enough to arrive
like a kiss on the wind, still fresh.

HANNAH HODGSON
Dancing with a Doctor

She tried to dance with me until I fainted.
I saw it then, the medical flickering,
making her face a lighter. She remembers
my body as a candlestick, that I'm nearly spent

and she tries to scrape the wax of me
off the windowsill. Others gather,
of course they do. The medical is contagious.
They know the heat I'm exuding, heat

that can't be stopped from rising. Tonight,
I want them to forget I'm a cardiac arrhythmia,
forget I'm a venous system, forget I'm necrotic tissue.
Tonight, I am sequins. I'm a lost clutch bag.

I'm a pay-as-you-go mobile. These items
don't need a doctor. All I need is a full fat coke
and maybe a vodka. I need forgetting,
a loss of the conscious medical. I need her

to be a clueless civilian; questioning
if smelling salts work, if she should raise my legs;
if she should call an ambulance. She shouldn't search
for my carotid, for the stitching of my heart.

Tonight, she must remember I am sequins.
Yes, a pulse, and she makes it quicken.

KWAME DAWES

Keratoconus

I cherish now all of light's fruitfulness,
this day of wars and quakes under the mute sun;
I repeat my songs of gratitude for being blessed,
and it seems like ingratitude for me to run
to that dark year I looked up to the trees
and saw what looked like streaks blurring the core
of the earth. That year, the doctors said shells
covered my cornea. They asked me to say more
about family history – the blindness, the bees
eating away at our light. All sight ceased that year.
I became a poet who sees through dying cells.

AARON KENT

Scabies vs Predator

The sky is on fire.
The light of the sun seems too big.
It is falling through the ceiling
to the floor
and the whole ceiling seems to be on fire,
and the basement and the family room,
and the entire bathroom
and my living room
and my bedroom
and the stairwell and the kitchen are on fire.
Everything is in slow motion.
Everything is a pool of fire and smoke.

There is nothing in the universe
but a seething, engulfing ocean of flame.
And then the universe turns into a diamond.

The sun is a diamond.
The sky is a diamond.
The air is a diamond.
The moon is a diamond.
The planets are diamonds.
The constellations are diamonds.

There is nothing in the universe
but a seething, engulfing ocean of diamonds
and, just as the diamonds become suns
I wake up.

My bed is surrounded by snoring stray cats.
I have a single sheet on the bed and my quilt is on the floor.
I'm covered in cat hair, my shirt is sticking to me,
my skin is stuck to my sheets.
I crawl across the floor to my bathtub.
I get in and wash myself with snow.
I wash myself with snow.

NAT RAHA

[subterranean / dreaming grace roots]

subterranean
   dreaming grace roots
               we feast from (:)
  calls your hand tender
        turned toward the margins
  in which we
       stir ancestral / souls
  against hegemonic

         nerves

  with what found & forged love ,
       if in alignment our /
 bodies defy
all the social could expect

 run seams im/possibility

& all the flesh we've
  fought for
    & the ways of being &
      knowing & fucking

       on history's tide
      receding , sure tears,
         façades
    horror , food ,

umber busy pulling
out of the ordinary, demands
, antinomies, borders
in the composition of hands

re:visioning
lay ripe heads as the sun
thins

dizzy scent's course
to place cupped on the chest
for a kinetics of otherwise

JOSEPHINE DICKINSON

Alphabetula

ASECRETPLACEMADEOFWORDSANCAORANANAEROBICā
cBUGHABURNTHILLBIERCEBLāBēAMBEONETBREATHINGB
LARMÒNACHBOGACHBAITINEACHBLÀRBRUACHBRUGBÁI
SÍNBOGLACHBOGLETBROCHANBREUNLOCHCURHAGHC
RAGEECEALDCūCILCAOCHCARCAIRCANACHCORRACHCR
AICCMIRCOKELAYKDIDDERDYANDEDWFRDEEPDUBEROS
IONEANACHFLASSFLASSHEFLOSSHEFLOTFUGOLFYRHTHEF
EITHFRIDDFIANACHFIZMERFOGAGGEYFOGGITFRAOCHFL
OWGRUGOGGLISTEGOLAGOTTYGADSHASSOCKHAGGY
HARPHAUGRHEWHRīSHEAWANHOGGHUSSOCKHAEGHūSI
CEJUNIPERUSKIARRKRINGLALāWERCELOWNLÒNLÈIGCH
RUTHAICHMOSSFLATSMANDALAMōRMOSIMYRRMIGNMA
WNMÒINEDHUBHMÒINTEACHMOSSMOTEMUMPNETHER
HEARTHSIKENAUTNEARUOGLENORGANICOXAPHLOEMP
OLLPEATPIPRAKEICEPLUMPEPLOMPEPOTPWLLPAETHPEEWI
TLANDPLIMPYLLAQUACKYQUAGMIREQUICKFRESHQUE
RCUSRūHSICRIONNACHMAOIMMACKERELRIOTRÁREIKRI
VELINGROSRÙSGRAONROSSSUNDORSELJASCēAPSTUBBST
RATIGRAPHICSPONGESSKARTHSEALHSAUTHRSEFSīCSÍKSÍO
NSÍSKÓGRSUNTSWANGSīDESTUGGEDSKALLISLACKSLUNK
TITEITOTTTRUNTUFTTUSKTIMBRTRODTEINEBIORACHU
PPEUNCONSCIOUSUFERAVEGGSVONDRVIDDAVRÁWAEF
REWAETERWATTERWELIGWENTWITHIGWUDUWIELLEWY
RMWHAMWINDWALEEXYLEMYARFYARPHAZAMZODY

JANE KENYON

Having It Out with Melancholy

> If many remedies are prescribed for an illness,
> you may be certain that the illness has no cure.
>
> A.P. CHEKHOV
> *The Cherry Orchard*

1 *From the Nursery*

When I was born, you waited
behind a pile of linen in the nursery,
and when we were alone, you lay down
on top of me, pressing
the bile of desolation into every pore.

And from that day on
everything under the sun and moon
made me sad – even the yellow
wooden beads that slid and spun
along a spindle on my crib.

You taught me to exist without gratitude.
You ruined my manners toward God:
'We're here simply to wait for death;
the pleasures of earth are overrated.'

I only appeared to belong to my mother,
to live among blocks and cotton undershirts
with snaps; among red tin lunch boxes
and report cards in ugly brown slipcases.
I was already yours – the anti-urge,
the mutilator of souls.

2 *Bottles*

Elavil, Ludiomil, Doxepin,
Norpramin, Prozac, Lithium, Xanax,
Wellbutrin, Parnate, Nardil, Zoloft.
The coated ones smell sweet or have
no smell; the powdery ones smell
like the chemistry lab at school
that made me hold my breath.

3 *Suggestion from a Friend*

You wouldn't be so depressed
if you really believed in God.

4 *Often*

Often I go to bed as soon after dinner
as seems adult
(I mean I try to wait for dark)
in order to push away
from the massive pain in sleep's
frail wicker coracle.

5 *Once There Was Light*

Once, in my early thirties, I saw
that I was a speck of light in the great
river of light that undulates through time.

I was floating with the whole
human family. We were all colors – those
who are living now, those who have died,
those who are not yet born. For a few

moments I floated, completely calm,
and I no longer hated having to exist.

Like a crow who smells hot blood
you came flying to pull me out
of the glowing stream.
'I'll hold you up. I never let my dear
ones drown!' After that, I wept for days.

6   *In and Out*

The dog searches until he finds me
upstairs, lies down with a clatter
of elbows, puts his head on my foot.

Sometimes the sound of his breathing
saves my life – in and out, in
and out; a pause, a long sigh …

7   *Pardon*

A piece of burned meat
wears my clothes, speaks
in my voice, dispatches obligations
haltingly, or not at all.
It is tired of trying

to be stouthearted, tired
beyond measure.

We move on to the monoamine
oxidase inhibitors. Day and night
I feel as if I had drunk six cups
of coffee, but the pain stops
abruptly. With the wonder
and bitterness of someone pardoned
for a crime she did not commit
I come back to marriage and friends,
to pink-fringed hollyhocks; come back
to my desk, books, and chair.

8 *Credo*

Pharmaceutical wonders are at work
but I believe only in this moment
of well-being. Unholy ghost,
you are certain to come again.

Coarse, mean, you'll put your feet
on the coffee table, lean back,
and turn me into someone who can't
take the trouble to speak; someone
who can't sleep, or who does nothing
but sleep; can't read, or call
for an appointment for help.

There is nothing I can do
against your coming.
When I awake, I am still with thee.

9 *Wood Thrush*

High on Nardil and June light
I wake at four,
waiting greedily for the first
note of the wood thrush. Easeful air
presses through the screen
with the wild, complex song
of the bird, and I am overcome

by ordinary contentment.
What hurt me so terribly
all my life until this moment?
How I love the small, swiftly
beating heart of the bird
singing in the great maples;
its bright, unequivocal eye.

PASCALE PETIT
Bac du Sauvage

Not the ferry itself across the Petit Rhône
nor the narrow road between the river
and the canal through marsh leading to it,

not the low powerlines like bunting
along one side, with songbirds silhouetted
against the sun on this savage land.

Not even when, if we stared at them long enough,
their colours would reveal them to be
bee-eaters scanning the sky for insects.

Not how, when we reached the barge, we turned
back to be on the right side of the road,
closer to them, as if we could catch our lives

in our mouths as easily as they snatched
wasps in their flight. As if we could stop
the car and snap them up with our camera,

take their quintessence home, then peer
at the shots for glints of us in their red eyes.
No, not even how beautiful we could be

in chestnut, gold and turquoise raiment
reflecting tints of the atlas
as we migrate across the hungry globe –

what if we could rub all the world's harms
from the air as they do, dash hornets' tails
against the post, until their stings break off?

MAYA ABU AL-HAYYAT

You Can't

They will fall in the end,
those who say you can't.
It'll be age or boredom that overtakes them,
or lack of imagination.
Sooner or later, all leaves fall to the ground.
You can be the last leaf.
You can convince the universe
that you pose no threat
to the tree's life.

translated from the Arabic by Fady Joudah

BIOGRAPHICAL NOTES

Iyanuoluwa Adenle is a writer living in Lagos, Nigeria. She is curious about how memory, time and place work, and how we navigate life with language as a witness. Her works make a conscious attempt to explore the human condition based on grief, loss, and love. Her writings have appeared or are forthcoming in *Agbowo, Banshee Lit, Maroko, Peppercoast Lit, Olongo, Lolwe*, and elsewhere.

Ekiwah Adler-Beléndez is from Amatlan, Mexico. He is the author of five collections of poetry, *Soy* (I Am); *Palabras Inagotables* (Never-ending Words); and *Weaver*, his first book in English; *The Coyote's Trace*, with an introduction by Mary Oliver. His latest work, *Love on Wheels*, deals with the richness and complexities of life in a wheelchair, and explores the relationship between poetry, disability and sexuality. He received the George Garrett Award for Distinguished Teaching in 2019. Website: www.ekiwahadler-belendez.net

Agha Shahid Ali (1949–2001) was a Kashmiri-American writer, born in New Delhi. He emigrated to the US in 1976 and later taught at the University of Utah, the MFA Program for Writers at Warren Wilson College and the University of Massachusetts. His collection, *Rooms Are Never Finished*, was a finalist for the National Book Awards in 2001. His translations include the poems of Mahmoud Darwish, Faiz Ahmed Faiz and Mirza Ghalib.

Sandra Alland is a writer and artist shielding in Glasgow. San's work examines qrip audiences and languages, integrated access and political mourning. For 25 years San has revelled in avant-garde poetry and stories, film performances, audio experiments and multimedia essays, presenting across Turtle Island, the UK, Europe and the internet. Books include *Anything Not Measurable Is Not Real* (Proper Tales, Cobourg), *Sore Loser* (with Etzali Hernández, Glasgow), *Naturally Speaking* (espresso, Tkaronto) and *Blissful Times* (Book*hug, Tkaronto). www.blissfultimes.ca

Shahd Alshammari is Associate Professor of English literature at Gulf University of Science and Technology in Kuwait. She is the author of *Head Above Water: Reflections on Illness* (Feminist Press).

JK Anowe (he/they) is an Igbo-born poet, editor, and teacher based in the USA. They are the author of the poetry chapbook *Sky Raining Fists* (Madhouse Press, 2019). Anowe has served as assistant poetry editor at *The Nation*, poetry editor of *Sycamore Review*, and poetry chapbooks editor for *Praxis Magazine*. A Gwendolyn M. Carter Fellow in African Studies at North-western University, Anowe is an MFA+MA candidate at the Litowitz Creative Writing Program. Anowe is completing a full-length collection of poems.

Raymond Antrobus is the author of *To Sweeten Bitter*, *The Perseverance*, *All the Names Given* and *Signs, Music*. Several of his poems were added to the GCSE syllabus in 2022. His picture books, *Can Bears Ski?* and *Terrible Horses,* are published by Walker Books. He is an advocate for several D/deaf charities including Deaf Kidz International and the National Deaf Children's Society.

Polly Atkin, FRSL, is a poet and nonfiction writer based in Cumbria. Her poetry collections are *Basic Nest Architecture* (Seren, 2017) and *Much With Body* (Seren, 2021). Her nonfiction includes *Recovering Dorothy: The Hidden Life of Dorothy Wordsworth* (Saraband, 2021), *Some Of Us Just Fall: On Nature and Not Getting Better* (Sceptre, 2023) and *The Company of Owls* (Elliott and Thompson, 2024). Her writing on nature and disability is also included in various anthologies, including *Moving Mountains* (Footnote, 2023).

Dean Atta is an award-winning Black British poet of Greek Cypriot and Jamaican heritage. He was listed as one of the most influential LGBTQIA+ people in the UK by the *Independent on Sunday*. He is the author of *I Am Nobody's Nigger*, shortlisted for the Polari First Book Prize; a young-adult novel in verse, *The Black Flamingo*; a picture book, *Confetti*; and a work of adult non-fiction, *Person Unlimited: An Ode to My Black Queer Body*.

Urvashi Bahuguna is an Indian poet and essayist whose work has been recognised by a Charles Wallace India Trust Fellowship, a Sangam House fellowship, an Eclectica Spotlight Author Prize, and a TOTO Award for Creative Writing. She is the author of a poetry collection, *Terrarium* (The (Great) Indian Poetry Collective, 2019), and a collection of personal essays on mental health, *No Straight Thing Was Ever Made* (Penguin Random House, 2021).

Abdullah al-Baradouni (1929–99) was a renowned Yemeni writer who contributed greatly to the rising of Arabic poetry. He published twelve poetry collections as well as books on politics, folklore and literature, receiving many awards. He become blind due to smallpox aged six, and later developed an encyclopaedic memory for poetry. He was arrested and imprisoned several times for his satirical poems. He was one of the first to call for a Union for Yemeni Authors and was its first chairman.

Khairani Barokka is a writer, artist, and editor from Jakarta. Okka's work has been presented widely internationally, and centres disability justice as anticolonial praxis. Among her honours, she's been a UNFPA Indonesian Young Leader Driving Social Change, a Delfina Foundation Associate Artist, an Artforum Must-See, Associate Artist at the UK's National Centre for Writing, and a shortlistee for the 2023 Asian Women of Achievement Awards. Her latest book is *amuk* (Nine Arches, 2024).

Kay Ulanday Barrett is a poet, essayist, cultural strategist, and A+ napper, navigating life as a disabled pilipinx-amerikan transgender queer in the U.S. with struggle, resistance, and laughter. Their second book, *More Than Organs* (Sibling Rivalry Press, 2020) received a 2021 Stonewall Honor Book Award by the American Library Association. Other awards include the 2022 Foundation for Contemporary Arts Cy Twombly Award for Poetry. For more info: kaybarrett.net & @Brownroundboi on social media.

Levent Beşkardèş is a multidisciplinary Deaf artist who creates poems in French Sign Language (LSF) and Turkish. He was born in Eskişehir,

Turkey, and has lived in France since 1980. A poet, actor, director, and visual artist, he has performed at the International Visual Theatre in Paris and has been a featured performer in festivals around the world. He has appeared in a number of films, including *J'avancerai vers toi avec les yeux d'un sourd* (2015). In 2010, he won the Honorary Prize of the Grand National Assembly of Turkey.

Brandi Bird is an Indigiqueer Saulteaux, Cree and Métis writer from Treaty 1 territory. Their chapbook, *I Am Still Too Much*, was published in 2019 by Rahila's Ghost Press. *The All + Flesh* was published by House of Anansi Press in 2023 and won the 2024 Indigenous Voices Award. They are a freelance editor, workshop facilitator and student of Creative Writing at the University of British Columbia.

Erez Bitton is an Israeli poet of Moroccan descent. At the age of 10, he lost his vision and left hand to a stray bomb and spent the rest of his childhood in Jerusalem's School for the Blind. His first two books revolutionised Hebrew literature and established him as the founding father of Mizrahi poetry. Bitton served as chairman of the Hebrew Writers Association, and is editor-in-chief of *Apyrion*, which he founded in 1982. *Shattered Rhymes*, a film about his life and poetry was produced by Sami Shalom Chetrit.

Jean 'Binta' Breeze (1956-2021) was an internationally renowned Jamaican Dub poet and storyteller whose performances were so powerful she was called a 'one-woman festival'. She published eight books of poetry and stories, and released several records, cassettes and CDs. She performed her work throughout the world, including tours of the Caribbean, Britain, North America, Europe, South East Asia and Africa. She received a NESTA Award in 2003, and an MBE in 2012 for services to literature.

Jane Burn is an award-winning poet, artist and hybrid writer. She is a working-class person with autism who lives with chronic pain and fatigue as a result of fibromyalgia/arthritis. Her work is widely published and anthologised. Her current collection, *The Apothecary of Flight*, is published by Nine Arches. She was the Michael Marks Awards Environmental Poet of the Year 2023/24, and lives off-grid in Northumberland for nine months of the year.

Madailín Burnhope is a Warwickshire-based queer, transfeminine poet with Spina Bifida, Hydrocephalus and EUPD. Her work has appeared in places like *Magma*, *Under The Radar*, *Ink Sweat and Tears*, *Gallus*, *Poetry Wales*, *Best British Poetry 2011* (Salt) and *Stairs and Whispers: D/deaf and Disabled Poets Write Back* (Nine Arches, 2017). Her debut collection was *Species* (Nine Arches, 2014). She is currently developing *A Miniature Book of Monsters* with mentor and Seren Books editor Zoë Brigley.

Jen Campbell is an award-winning poet and bestselling author of twelve books for adults and children. Her books have been translated into over twenty languages. She has won both the Jane Martin Poetry Prize and an Eric Gregory Award. Her first book-length collection, *The Girl Aquarium*, was published by Bloodaxe Books in 2019. *Please Do Not Touch This Exhibit* (Bloodaxe Books, 2023), was a Poetry Book Society Recommendation. Find out more at: www.jen-campbell.co.uk

Anthony Vahni Capildeo, FRSL, is a Trinidadian Scottish writer of poetry and non-fiction. Currently Writer in Residence and Professor at the University of York, their interests include silence, plurilingualism, place, memory, faith and traditional masquerade. *Polkadot Wounds* (Carcanet, 2024), their ninth full-length book, includes lyric techniques related to their experience of cPTSD and migraine.

Paul Celan (1920–70) is among the most important German-language poets of the 20th century. Born in Romania in 1920 into a German-speaking Jewish family, his parents were murdered in the Holocaust. He escaped a forced labour camp, eventually settling in Paris in 1948. The same year *Der Sand aus den Urnen* was published in Vienna, containing one of his best-known poems, 'Todesfuge' ('Death Fugue'). He translated French, Italian, and Russian poetry, as well as Shakespeare, into German. He died by suicide in 1970 after experiencing a series of psychotic episodes.

Cat Chong (they/them) is a poet, essayist and publisher from Singapore who completed their PhD at Nanyang Technological University, where their work considered the intersections between gender, genre and disability in contemporary experimental poetics. Their debut collection *712 stanza homes for the sun* was published in 2023 by Broken Sleep Books, and their second collection, the serial poem titled *Dear Lettera 32*, was released by Permeable Barrier in 2024.

John Lee Clark is a DeafBlind poet, essayist, translator, historian and Protactile educator. His book of poems, *How to Communicate*, won the Minnesota Book Award and a finalist for the National Book Award. His latest book is *Touch the Future: A Manifesto in Essays*. Originally from Minnesota, he now lives in Montreal, where he is the Miriam Roland Aaron Graduate Fellow at Concordia University.

Kate Davis is a poet and storyteller. She was born in 1951 on the Furness peninsula of south Cumbria and has always lived there. Her poems have been published in *Iota* and *Butcher's Dog*, implanted in audio-benches, sung throughout a 12-hour tide cycle, embroidered on clothes, remixed by a sound artist and printed on shopping bags. In 2013 she received a Northern Writers' Award, New Poets Bursary.

Kwame Dawes, FRSL, is the Poet Laureate of Jamaica. He is the author of 22 books of poetry and numerous books of fiction, criticism and essays. He is Glenna Luschei Editor-in-Chief of *Prairie Schooner* and George W. Holmes University Professor at the University of Nebraska, and a chancellor of the Academy of American Poets. His awards include an Emmy, a Guggenheim Fellowship, and the Windham Campbell Prize for poetry.

Deaf, genderqueer poet **Meg Day** is the author of *Last Psalm at Sea Level* (Barrow Street, 2014) and co-editor of *Laura Hershey: On the Life & Work of an American Master* (Pleiades, 2019). Day is the 2024 Guggenheim Poet-in-Residence, a recipient of the Amy Lowell Traveling Scholarship, and an NEA fellow; Day's work can be found in *Best American Poetry* and *The New York Times*. Day teaches in the MFA program at North Carolina State University. www.megday.com

Profoundly deaf overnight at the age of six, **Josephine Dickinson** entered the language poetry. Encouraged by the editor of her school magazine, she gained a place, from a poor working-class background, to read Classics at Oxford. After practice as a music teacher and composer, and moving to Cumbria, she published poetry collections and has another collection and a memoir in gestation. In between have been collaborations with musicians, artists and writers, and political campaigning.

Ali Cobby Eckermann is a Yankunytjatjara poet whose first collections, *little bit long time* and *Kami* (both 2010), quickly sold out their first print runs. She has published verse novels and a memoir, *Too Afraid to Cry*. She founded the first Aboriginal Writers Retreat in Koolunga. In 2017 Ali won the Windham Campbell Prize, and in 2024, the NSW Premier's Literary Awards Book of the Year and the Indigenous Writers' Prize for her third verse novel *She Is the Earth.*

Anita Endrezze is a writer, poet, teacher, and artist. Her work has been translated into ten languages (Farsi, Danish, French, German, Italian, Macedonian, Portuguese, Chinese, Catalan and Spanish). She has won the Washington State Writers Award, the Bumbershoot/Weyerhaeuser Award, an Artist Trust Gap Award, and the Washington Poetry Society Contest. Her writing appears in dozens of anthologies and her art has been exhibited around the globe. Born in Long Beach, California, Anita is half-Yaqui Indian, Slovenian, north Italian, German-Swiss.

Therese Estacion is the author of *Phantompains* (Book*hug Press) – a collection of poems that explores her Filipinx heritage and disability. *Phantompains* was a finalist for both the 2021 Indies Foreword Reviews and 2021 CLMP Firecracker Award. She has been a guest editor for *Arc* and curated Smutburger's 2023-2024 series. Therese currently teaches poetry at the University of Toronto's School of Continuing Studies and is training to be a psychotherapist.

Megan Fernandes is a South Asian American writer, author of *Good Boys* and *I Do Everything I'm Told*, both from Tin House Books. She was a finalist for the Kundiman Poetry Prize and the Paterson Poetry

Prize. Her poems have been published in *The New Yorker*, *Kenyon Review*, *Chicago Review*, *The American Poetry Review* and *Ploughshares*, and by the Academy of American Poets among others. She is associate professor of English and writer-in-residence at Lafayette College.

Janet Frame (1924-2004) published eleven novels, five collections of stories, a children's book and a three-volume autobiography, adapted by Jane Campion into her film *An Angel at My Table*, which told the story of how misdiagnosis as schizophrenic led to her spending years being poorly treated in psychiatric hospitals. Her poetry was published by Bloodaxe in the UK in *Storms Will Tell: Selected Poems*. She was made a CBE in 1983 for services to literature, and was made a Member of the Order of New Zealand. in 1990, New Zealand's highest civil honour.

Kathryn Gray lives in London. Recipient of an Eric Gregory Award, her first collection, *The Never-Never* (Seren, 2004), was shortlisted for the T.S. Eliot Prize and the Forward Prize for Best First Collection. An artist's book with Mary Modeen, *Uncertain Territories*, appeared in 2011; a pamphlet, *Flowers*, was published by Rack Press in 2016. Her second full collection, *Hollywood or Home* (Seren), was selected as a *Sunday Times* Poetry Book of the Year in 2023.

torrin a. greathouse (she/they) is a transgender cripple-punk, an MFA candidate at the University of Minnesota, and a 2021 National Endowment for the Arts Fellow. In 2020, she received fellowships from Zoeglossia and the University of Arizona Poetry Center. Her work is published in *Poetry*, *Ploughshares* and *The Kenyon Review*. Her debut collection *Wound from the Mouth of a Wound* was published by Milkweed Editions in 2020.

Ona Gritz's poems have appeared in *Ploughshares*, *Bellevue Literary Review*, *Catamaran Literary Reader* and *One Art*. Her most recent books are *Everywhere I Look*, a Readers' Choice Gold Award and Pencraft Best Book Award winner in memoir, and two YA verse novels, *The Space You Left Behind*, which was featured in The Children's Book Council's Hot Off the Press roundup of anticipated bestsellers, and *Take a Sad Song*, which earned a *Kirkus* starred review.

Marilyn Hacker is the author of 19 books of poems, including *Calligraphies* (Norton, 2023) and *Blazons* (Carcanet, 2019), co-author of two collaborative books, *DiaspoRenga*, written with Deema K. Shehabi, and *A Different Distance*, and translator of 23 books by French and Francophone poets, including Samira Negrouche, Claire Malroux and Vénus Khoury-Ghata. She lives in New York and Paris.

Golan Haji is a Syrian-Kurdish poet, essayist and translator with a postgraduate degree in pathology. He lives in France. He has published five books of poems in Arabic, most recently, *Scale of Injury* (2016) and *The Word Rejected* (2023). His poems have appeared in several languages and his translations include books by Robert Louis Stevenson and Alberto Manguel. He has also published *Until the War* (2016), a book of prose based on interviews with Syrian women.

Jamie Hale is a poet and multidisciplinary creative. Entangling nature, technology, and progressive impairment, their work asks what it means to be human. Jamie was a 2021-22 Jerwood Poetry Fellow, and winner of the *Evening Standard* Theatremaker of the Year 2021 for their poetry show, NOT DYING. Their pamphlet, *Shield*, was published by Verve in 2021, and they are finishing their first collection. Jamie also founded the award-winning CRIPtic Arts in 2019, and the Disabled Poets' Prize in 2023.

Kerry Hardie is an Irish poet and novelist, living with ME. Born in Singapore, she grew up in Co. Down, and lives in Co. Kilkenny in Ireland. Her poems have featured in *The Penguin Book of Irish Poetry* (2010) and *The Wake Forest Book of Irish Women's Poetry* (2011) as well as in ten Bloodaxe anthologies. Her ninth collection, *We Go On*, was published by Bloodaxe in 2024. Kerry Hardie is a member of Aosdána.

Born in 1980 in Lebanon, **Maya Abu al-Hayyat** is an Arabic-language Palestinian novelist, poet and children's book author who lives in Jerusalem and works in Ramallah. Fady Joudah's translation of her poetry, *You Can Be the Last Leaf*, was a finalist for the National Book Critics Circle Award. Her most recent novel is *No One Knows Their*

Blood Type. She is director of the Palestine Writing Workshop which seeks to encourage reading in Palestinian communities through creative writing projects and storytelling with children and teachers.

Stephanie Heit (she/her) is a queer disabled poet, dancer, teacher, and co-director of Turtle Disco, a somatic writing space on Anishinaabe land in Ypsilanti, Michigan. She is bipolar, a mad activist, a shock/psych system survivor, and a member of the Olimpias, an international disability performance collective. Her poetry collections are the book of hybrid memoir poems, *PSYCH MURDERS* (Wayne State University Press, 2022), and *The Color She Gave Gravity* (Operating System, 2017). Website: stephanie-heit.com

Selima Hill grew up in a family of painters on farms in England and Wales, and has lived in Dorset for the past 40 years. Her 22nd book of poetry, *A Man, a Woman and a Hippopotamus*, is published by Bloodaxe Books in 2025. Hill was awarded The King's Gold Medal for Poetry, 2022, made on the basis of her body of work, with special recognition for her 2008 Bloodaxe Books retrospective *Gloria: Selected Poems*.

Hannah Hodgson is an award-winning poet, writer, palliative care patient and advisory consultant. She is the recipient of two Northern Writers Awards for Poetry, and the Poetry Business New Poets Prize. In recognition of her activism, Hannah received a prestigious Diana Legacy Award in 2021, given in the name of Diana, Princess of Wales. Only 20 are given out worldwide biannually. *163 Days* was published by Seren in 2022 and adapted into a play for BBC Sounds. www.hannahhodgson.com

A Chickasaw poet, novelist, essayist and environmentalist, **Linda Hogan** was born in Denver, Colorado. Active as an educator and speaker, she has been a speaker at the United Nations Forum and was a plenary speaker at the Environmental Literature Conference in Turkey in 2009. Hogan's awards include a Lannan Literary Award and a Lifetime Achievement Award from the Native Writers Circle of the Americas. In 2016 she was awarded the Thoreau Prize from PEN.

Mishka Hoosen was born and raised in Newclare, Johannesburg, and graduated from UCKAR's MA in Creative Writing program with distinction. Her first chapbook of poetry, *Road Trip with James Dean*, was published in 2011 by Flomotion. Her poetry has been performed across South Africa, and in Ireland and the United States. She is physically disabled, mentally ill, and autistic. She is currently working on a second novel, writing about perfume, memory, and the senses.

Cynthia Huntington is the author of several collections of poetry, including *Fire Muse: Poems from the Salt House* (2016); *Heavenly Bodies* (2012), nominated for a National Book Award; Levis Prize-winner, *The Radiant* (2003); as well as the nonfiction prose volume *The Salt House* (1998). A former poet laureate of New Hampshire, she chaired the poetry jury for the 2006 Pulitzer Prize in Poetry. She is a professor of English and creative writing at Dartmouth College, New Hampshire.

Shiki Itsuma (1917-59) developed leprosy at 13 and spent the rest of his life in leprosy hospitals, slowly losing use of his hands, then his feet. He converted to Christianity in 1942. His poems were widely published in magazines and anthologies during his lifetime, but not collected until a year after his death. Shiki was a significant influence in changing the perception of so-called leprosy literature, which became its own genre in Japan.

Andy Jackson is a disabled poet, essayist, creative writing teacher at the University of Melbourne, and a Patron of Writers Victoria. His latest poetry collection is *Human Looking*, which won the ALS Gold Medal and the Prime Minister's Literary Award for Poetry. Andy is a co-editor of *Raging Grace: Australian Writers Speak Out on Disability* (Puncher & Wattman, 2024), an anthology of collaborative poems and essays. He writes and rests on Dja Dja Wurrung country.

Cyrée Jarelle Johnson (he/him) is a poet and writer from Piscataway, NJ. His work has appeared in *The New York Times*, *Yale Review*, *Granta*, *Poetry*, and Academy of American Poets *Poem-A-Day*, among other publications. He is the author of award-winning collections, *WATCH-*

NIGHT and *SLINGSHOT*, both with Nightboat Books, and recipient of a 2023 Creative Writing Fellowship from the National Endowment for the Arts, and a 2020 Ruth Lilly & Dorothy Sargent Rosenberg Poetry Fellowship from the Poetry Foundation.

Rachael Johnson is a disabled, neurodivergent Diné writer/poet/photographer from the Navajo Nation. She belongs to Táchii'nii, the Red Running into the Water people, and is born for Kinyaa'áanii, the Towering House clan. *The Diné Reader: An Anthology of Navajo Literature,* in which her poems were published, received a 2022 Before Columbus Foundation American Book Award. Her poetry/photography chapbook, *My Body is an Ill-fitting Costume*, was published by Abalone Mountain Press in 2023.

I.S. Jones is an American / Nigerian poet and editor. She is a senior editor for *Poetry Northwest* where she runs her column, *The Legacy Suite*, a three-part interview documenting the journey of writers publishing their debut poetry collections. Her chapbook *Spells of My Name* (2021) was selected by Newfound for their Emerging Poets Series.

Ilya Kaminsky was born in Ukraine and now lives in the USA. He is the author of *Deaf Republic* and *Dancing in Odessa*, both published in the UK by Faber.

Lisa Kelly is a poet, editor and educator based in London. She has single-sided deafness and is half Danish. Her second collection, *The House of the Interpreter* (Carcanet), was a Poetry Book Society Recommendation. Her first collection, *A Map Towards Fluency* (Carcanet), was shortlisted for the Michael Murphy Memorial Poetry Prize 2021. She co-edited the anthology, *What Meets the Eye?: The Deaf Perspective* (Arachne Press, 2021). She is Chair of Magma Poetry.

Gayle Kennedy is a member of the Wongaiibon Clan of New South Wales in Australia, and was Indigenous Issues editor and writer for Streetwise Comics from 1995 to 1998. In 2005 her book of poetry *Koori Girl Goes Shoppin'* was shortlisted for the David Unaipon Award, and in 2006 she won the David Unaipon Award for *Me, Antman & Fleabag*. Gayle has published eleven children's books as part of OUP's Yarning Strong series, and six of these were nominated for the 2011 Deadly Award for Achievement in Literature.

Aaron Kent is a working-class writer, stroke survivor and insomniac from Cornwall. His second poetry collection, *The Working Classic*, is available from the87press, and his debut, *Angels the Size of Houses*, from Shearsman. He has read his poetry for the BBC, the Shakespeare Birthplace Trust, and Stroke Association, and is an Arvon tutor. His poetry has been translated into languages including French, Hungarian, German, Cymraeg and Kernewek, and has been set to music.

Jane Kenyon (1947–95) was born in Michigan and grew up in the Midwest. She attended the University of Michigan and in 1972 married the poet Donald Hall, whom she met while a student. Kenyon published four books of poetry: *Constance* (1993), *Let Evening Come* (1990), *The Boat of Quiet Hours* (1986), and *From Room to Room* (1978), and a book of translation, *Twenty Poems of Anna Akhmatova* (1985). She was named poet laureate of New Hampshire in 1995, but died later that year from leukaemia. Her UK retrospective, *Let Evening Come: Selected Poems* (2005), is available from Bloodaxe.

Karl Knights' poems, journalism and essays have appeared in *The Guardian*, *The Poetry Review*, *The Rialto*, *The Dark Horse* and elsewhere. He won the 2021 New Poets Prize. His debut pamphlet, *Kin*, appeared with The Poetry Business in 2022. He lives in Suffolk.

Petra Kuppers (she/her) is a disability culture activist, a scooter/wheelchair user, and a community performance artist. Her fourth poetry collection, *Diver Beneath the Street*, investigates true crime and eco-poetry at the level of the soil (Wayne State University Press, 2024). Her previous collection, *Gut Botany* (2020), won the 2021/22 Creative Book Award by the Association for the Study of Literature and the Environment. She teaches at the University of Michigan and was a 2023 Guggenheim Fellow.

Stephen Kuusisto is the author of *Eavesdropping: A Memoir of Blindness and Listening*; the acclaimed memoir *Planet of the Blind*, a *New York Times* Notable Book of the Year; and *Only Bread, Only Light* (Copper Canyon Press). Steve has appeared on programmes including *The Oprah Winfrey Show* and *Dateline NBC*, and on National Public Radio and the BBC. He is director of the Renée Crown University Honors Program at Syracuse University and speaks widely on diversity, disability, education and public policy.

Khando Langri is a hard-of-hearing Tibetan writer, poet and PhD candidate in anthropology at Stanford University. She loves writing about roads, mountains and golden fish.

Adrienne Leddy (they/them) is a mixed Indigenous Chamorro with chronic illness. They were born and raised in Yelamu (San Francisco, CA) and love the land that raised them. They are passionate about abolition and autonomy, harm reduction, sci-fi and fantasy, and spending time with their dog!

Gwyneth Lewis was Wales's inaugural National Poet and wrote the words on the front of the Wales Millennium Centre. An award-winning poet in both Welsh and English, she has written on depression *(Sunbathing in the Rain)* and emotional abuse in her memoir *Nightshade Mother* and poetry collection *First Rain in Paradise*. She was awarded an MBE for services to literature and mental health and suffers from chronic migraine.

Joanne Limburg's most recent poetry collection is *The Autistic Alice* (Bloodaxe Books). She has also published fiction and non-fiction, including *Letters to My Weird Sisters: On Autism and Feminism*. She lives in Cambridge and teaches creative writing at the Cambridge University Institute of Continuing Education.

Ada Limón is the author of six books of poetry, including *The Carrying*, which won the National Book Critics Circle Award for Poetry. Her most recent book, *The Hurting Kind*, was shortlisted for the Griffin Poetry Prize. She was the 24th Poet Laureate of the United States, the recipient of a MacArthur Fellowship, and a *TIME* magazine woman of the year. As Poet Laureate, her signature project was You Are Here, focusing on poetry and the natural world.

Sarah Lubala is a Congolese-born South Africa-based poet. When she was three, her family fled the Democratic Republic of Congo at a time of political unrest and communal violence, and she now suffers from chronic pain which she attributes to early traumas. After being short-listed twice for the Gerald Kraak Award and once for The Brittle Paper Poetry Award, she went on to win the HSS Award 2023 for Best Fiction: Poetry, and the Ingrid Jonker Prize 2024. Her debut collection, *A History of Disappearance*, was published by Botsotso Publishing in 2022.

Roddy Lumsden (1966–2020) was born in St Andrews, Scotland. He was a freelance writer, editor, influential teacher and mentor, and a writer of puzzles and quizzes for newspapers. He published nine collections of poetry, of which *The Book of Love* (Bloodaxe Books, 2000) and *So Glad I'm Me* (Bloodaxe Books, 2017) were shortlisted for the T.S. Eliot Prize. Roddy edited *Identity Parade*, an anthology of recent British and Irish poets (Bloodaxe Books, 2010).

Osip Mandelstam (1891–1938) grew up in St Petersburg. With Anna Akhmatova and Nikolai Gumilev he formed the Acmeist movement. In 1938 he was sentenced by the Stalinist regime to five years' hard labour for 'counter-revolutionary activities'. Suffering from torture-induced mental illness, he died that winter, of 'heart failure', in a freezing transit camp in Siberia. His poetry and prose have been called 'an extraordinary testament to the endurance of art in the presence of terror'.

Jack Mapanje is a Malawian writer, linguist and human rights activist. He was head of English at the Chancellor College, University of Malawi, before being imprisoned in 1987 for his collection *Of Chameleons and Gods*, which the dictator Hastings Banda read as a coded attack on himself. He was released in 1991, following an international outcry against his incarceration in brutal conditions, and emigrated to the UK, where he was able to receive medical treatment for his injuries. He lives in York.

Airea D. Matthews's debut collection, *Simulacra*, won the 2016 Yale Series of Younger Poets Prize. Her most recent collection, *Bread and Circus*, won the 2023 Los Angeles Times Book Prize for Poetry. She is a 2024 Guggenheim Fellow. Her poetry often explores identity, history, philosophy, and the intersections of personal and public life. She teaches creative writing at Bryn Mawr College in Pennsylvania.

Lateef McLeod is a poet, novelist, activist and scholar from Oakland, California. In 2019 he started the podcast *Black Disabled Men Talk*, with co-hosts Leroy Moore, Keith Jones and Ottis Smith. His books include *Studies in Brotherly Love* (Prompt Press, 2021), a collaborative ekphrastic-artist book; *Whispers of Krip Love Shouts of Krip Revolution* (Poetic Matrix Press, 2020); and *A Declaration of a Body of Love* (Atahualpa Press, 2009). McLeod co-authored *Supporting Individuals Who Use Augmentative and Alternative Communication* (Plural Publishing, 2022).

Erica Mena is a Puerto Rican poet, translator, and book artist. Their books include *Featherbone* (Ricochet Editions, 2015) and their translation of the Argentine graphic novel *The Eternaut* by H.G. Oesterheld and F. Solano Lopez (Fantagraphics, 2015). Their artist books are held in collections including at the Whitney Museum. They have taught Book Arts, Translation and Poetry at Brown University, Mills College, Harvard University, and elsewhere. They currently live in Fiskars, Finland. Find more at www.acyborgkitty.com

Kei Miller was born in Jamaica in 1978 and writes across a range of genres. His poetry collection, *The Cartographer Tries to Map a Way to Zion*, won the Forward Prize, while his novel, *Augustown*, won the Bocas Prize for Caribbean Literature, the Prix Les Afriques, and the Prix Carbet de la Caraïbe et du Tout-Monde. Honours include the Institute of Jamaica's Silver Musgrave medal and the Anthony Sabga medal for Arts & Letters. He is Professor of English at the University of Miami.

Leroy F. Moore Jr is an African American author/artist/activist, and a former founding member of National Black Disability Coalition and an activist around police brutality against people with disabilities.

191

Moore has started and helped start organisations including Disability Advocates of Minorities Organization, Sins Invalid, and Krip-Hop Nation. His cultural work includes the film documentary *Where Is Hope, Police Brutality Against People with Disabilities*, spoken-word CDs, poetry books and the children's book *Black Disabled Art History 101* (Xochitl Justice Press).

Tito Rajarshi Mukhopadhyay, a leading poet and memoirist of the experience of autism, was born in India in 1988. His work challenges conventional measures of mental states and abilities. Tito's life and work have been featured widely in the media, including *Sixty Minutes*, *Good Morning America*, *The New York Times*, *Scientific American*, *National Geographic*, PBS, CNN, BBC and *Disability Studies Quarterly*. He lives in Texas where his mother directs the autism organisation HALO. http://www.halo-soma.org

Les Murray (1938–2019) grew up on a dairy farm at Bunyah in New South Wales. He studied at Sydney University and later worked as a translator at the Australian National University and as an officer in the Prime Minister's Department. From 1971 until his death he made literature his full-time career. He was nominated for the Oxford Chair of Poetry in 1994 and was awarded the Queen's Gold Medal for Poetry for 1998. His many books include *Killing the Black Dog: a memoir of depression* (2011).

Karthika Naïr was born with RDEB inversa, a rare disorder of the skin and mucous membranes. Even minor friction – sneezes, handshakes – can result in erosions or blisters resembling third degree burns. When not combating triffids in hospital, she can usually be found around dance studios. Sometimes, that results in books (*A Different Distance, The Honey Hunter...*), sometimes in dance/theatre productions with colleagues (*Beneath the Music, ROOH, Mariposa...*). Sometimes, all of the above (*Until the Lions*). Originally from India, she lives in Paris.

Chisom Okafor is a Nigerian poet and clinical nutritionist, presently living in Alabama where he is an MFA in Creative Writing candidate and Graduate Council Fellow. His poems, which mostly explore his chronic illness, appear in *The Ending Hasn't Happened Yet*, an anthology of disabled and neurodivergent poets (ed. Hannah Soyer) and *In-Between Spaces: An Anthology of Disabled Writers* (ed. Rebecca Burke). He has received support from the Sundress Academy for the Arts and Commonwealth Foundation.

Frank Ormsby was born in 1947, in Enniskillen, Northern Ireland, and educated at Queen's University, Belfast. In 1992 he received the Cultural Traditions Award, and in 2002 the Lawrence O'Shaughnessy Award for Poetry from the University of St Thomas at St Paul, Minnesota. He was editor of *The Honest Ulsterman* from 1969 to 1989. His collection, *The Darkness of Snow* (Bloodaxe Books, 2017) contains a moving and humorous sequence on the early stages of Parkinson's Disease.

Naomi Ortiz (they/she) is the author of *Rituals for Climate Change: A Crip Struggle for Ecojustice* (2023) and *Sustaining Spirit: Self-Care for Social Justice* (2018). They are a 2022 U.S. Artists Disability Futures Fellow (Ford & Mellon Foundation) and a Reclaiming the U.S./Mexico Border Narrative Grant Awardee. Their widely published poetry, writing and visual art focuses on self-care, disability justice, and climate action in the Arizona U.S./Mexico borderlands. www.NaomiOrtiz.com

Saleem Hue Penny (him/friend) is a Black, disabled, 'rural hip-hop blues' poet who punctuates his hybrid/mixed media work with drum loops, Jim Crow artefacts and birch bark. A proud Cave Canem Fellow, 2024 Disability Futures Fellow, and a member of O|Sessions Black Listening cohort, Saleem edits at *Bellevue Literary Review* and was a 2021 Poetry Coalition Fellow. He is a worker-owner of Cooperation Racine in Englewood, Chicago.

Lucia Perillo (1958–2016) grew up in Manhattan. She was the recipient of many awards for her work and a finalist for the Pulitzer Prize. She was diagnosed with multiple sclerosis when she was in her 30s. Her collection of essays, *I've Heard the Vultures Singing* (2005), is a clear-eyed and brazenly outspoken examination of her life as a person with disabilities. She was awarded a prestigious MacArthur 'genius' grant in 2000.

Pascale Petit is a writer of French, Welsh, and Indian heritage. Her poetry collection, *Tiger Girl* (Bloodaxe Books, 2020), was shortlisted for the Forward Prize and for Wales Book of the Year. *Mama Amazonica* won the Laurel and Ondaatje prizes. Her first novel, *My Hummingbird Father*, was published by Salt in 2024, and her ninth collection, *Beast*, by Bloodaxe in 2025.

Leah Lakshmi Piepzna-Samarasinha (they/she) is a nonbinary femme autistic disabled writer, space creator and disability and transformative justice movement worker of Burgher and Tamil Sri Lankan, Irish and Galician/Roma descent. They are the author or co-editor of ten books, including *The Future Is Disabled: Prophecies, Love Notes and Mourning Songs*; *Tonguebreaker*; *Care Work: Dreaming Disability Justice*; and *Bodymap*. They are currently at work building Living Altars/The Stacey Park Milbern Liberation Arts Center, a home for disabled QTBIPOC writers. brownstargirl.org

Nat Raha is a poet and activist-scholar whose books include *Counter-sonnets* (Contraband Books, 2013), *sirens, body & faultlines* (Boiler House Press, 2018) and *apparitions (nines)* (Nightboat Books, 2024). Her work has appeared in *100 Queer Poems* (2022) and *We Want It All: An Anthology of Radical Trans Poetics* (2020), among others. With Mijke Van der Drift, she co-edits the *Radical Transfeminism* zine. She is Lecturer in Fine Art Critical Studies at the Glasgow School of Art.

heidi andrea restrepo rhodes (they/them) is a queer, gender fluid/trans, crip/disabled, brown, writer, artist, scholar, educator, cultural worker and creature of the Colombian diaspora. Their poetry collection, *The Inheritance of Haunting* (University of Notre Dame Press, 2019) won the 2018 Andrés Montoya Poetry Prize and their chapbook, *Ephemeral* (Ecotheo Collective, 2024) was awarded the 2022 Lorca Latinx Poetry Prize. They currently live in southern California.

G.N. Saibaba (1967–2024) was an Indian scholar, writer and human rights activist. He was born in Andhra Pradesh and used a wheelchair since the age of five due to polio. An assistant professor at Ram Lal Anand

College of Delhi University, Saibaba was wrongfully imprisoned in 2014 as part of the State's alleged 'crackdown' on Maoist activity. Despite repeated acquittals by regional courts in the country and pleas from international humanitarian organisations, he was denied bail and medical care, and wasn't released until 2024. He died seven months later, another fatal casualty of state-orchestrated injustice.

Riyad al-Saleh al-Hussein (1954–82) was a Syrian poet from Daraa, one of the most influential pioneers of modern Arabic poetry. He suffered throughout his short life from deafness, kidney failure and diabetes, and scrounged a meagre living working various menial jobs. During his brief lifetime, he published three poetry collections: *Failure of Circulation* (1979), *Daily Legends* (1980) and *Simple Like Water, Clear Like a Bullet* (1982). His fourth collection, *Bull in a Jungle*, was published posthumously.

Badr Shākir al-Sayyāb (1926–64) was born in a village near Basra, Iraq. He published seven collections of poetry in his lifetime and produced many works of translation. Frequently his subject was political and social oppression, as is evident in 'Rain Song', written while in exile in Kuwait and considered to be one of the greatest poems of modern Arabic poetry. He developed motor neuron disease, and then paralysis, continuing to write and publish up until his death.

Masaoka Shiki (1867–1902) was a Japanese poet, essayist, critic and diarist, considered to be one of the four great masters of Haiku poetry. He was also an innovator of the Tanka form. He was born in Matsuyama City in Iyo Province into a samurai family and attended the University of Tokyo but failed his finals due to being absorbed in writing poetry. He suffered from tuberculosis most of his life, developed Pott's Disease and was bedridden from 1897.

Born in Sydney in 1962, **Kerri Shying** is of Wiradjuri, Chinese and Scotch family. They live with disability in New South Wales, publishing four collections of poetry since 2017: *Sing out when you want me* (Flying Island/ASM, 2017), *Elevensies* (Puncher & Wattman, 2018), *Knitting Mangrove Roots* (Flying Island/ASM, 2019) and *Know Your Country*

(Puncher & Wattman, 2021). Their work is widely anthologised and they pioneered the poetic form 'elevensies' as a decolonising endeavour.

Daniel Sluman is a 38-year-old poet and disability rights activist. He co-edited the first major UK Disability poetry anthology, *Stairs and Whispers: D/deaf and Disabled Poets Write Back*, and has published three poetry collections with Nine Arches Press. His most recent collection, *single window* (2021), was shortlisted for the T.S. Eliot Prize.

Gaele Sobott is a writer striving to cultivate an indoor jungle and balcony garden in her apartment on Wangal land, Sydney. Her books include *Colour Me Blue*, a collection of short stories, and *My Longest Round*, a biography. She has published work in literary magazines and anthologies, and her poetry animations earn international acclaim. Gaele is the recipient of a 2023 Australia Council Fellowship, 2021 Varuna Writers' Space Fellowship, and 2020 City of Sydney Fellowship.

William Soutar (1898–1943) was born in Perth, Scotland, and attended the University of Edinburgh. During his time serving in the Royal Navy he contracted ankylosing spondylitis, rendering him bedridden from 1930 onwards. His first collection of poems in Scots were 'bairn-rhymes' for children. In 1935 he published *Poems in Scots*. After being diagnosed with tuberculosis he began writing a secret diary, published as *The Diary of a Dying Man* in 1954. Soutar is considered one of the finest Scottish poets of the 20th century.

Steffi Tad-y is the author of the poetry collection *From the Shoreline* (Gordon Hill Press, 2022), and two chapbooks, *I Did Not Want to Be Read* (2019) from Frog Hollow Press, and *Merienda* (2021) from Rahila's Ghost Press. Steffi's work reflects on kinship, diasporic geographies, and formations of the mind. Her work has garnered nominations from the bpNichol Chapbook Award and the Pat Lowther Memorial Prize. She is based in Vancouver, British Columbia.

At the age of 24, while teaching a gymnastics class, **Hoshino Tomihiro** (1946-2024) had an accident which left him quadriplegic. In hospital, he learnt to write and paint with a brush in his mouth, and began writing poetry. He also became a Christian; his faith was a strong influence in his writing. He was the author of 13 collections of picture-poems, as well as many other books. www.city.midori.gunma.jp/tomihiro/

Hàn Mặc Tử (1912–40) was a modernist poet from Vietnam who founded the 'Chaos' (Loạn) or 'Mad' (Điên) school of poetry after contracting leprosy. His work contributed greatly to the revitalisation of Classical verse with French influence. 'Đây Thôn Vĩ Dạ' ('Here in Vĩ Dạ Hamlet') (1938) is considered to be a masterpiece and an outstanding work of modern Vietnamese poetry. Around the time of writing, Hàn Mặc Tử was in intense pain, both physically and mentally.

Nuala Watt lives in Glasgow. Her poems have appeared in anthologies including *Stairs and Whispers: D/Deaf and Disabled Writers Write Back* (Nine Arches, 2017) and *A Year of Scottish Poems* (Pan Macmillan, 2018). She has been featured on BBC radio and on The Poetry Archive. Interests include visual impairment as a creative context and disabled parenthood. Her collection *The Department of Work and Pensions Assesses a Jade Fish* was published by Blue Diode in 2024.

David Wheatley is the author of six collections of poetry, including *Child Ballad* (2023). His neurodivergent novel *Stretto* was published by CB Editions in 2022. He lives in rural Aberdeenshire, Scotland.

Born in 1976 in Hengdian village, Hubei province, **Yu Xiuhua** is from an impoverished rural background. She has cerebral palsy. In 2014, her poem 'Crossing Half of China to Fuck You' became an online sensation, launching her career as a celebrity poet and writer. Her collection *Moonlight Rests on My Left Palm* (Guangxi Normal University Press, 2015) sold over eight hundred thousand copies, a record for Chinese poetry titles of the past three decades.

Zuo You is a Chinese poet based in Xi'an. His poems have appeared in some major literary magazines in China. Suffering from a hearing impairment, he can only speak a few simple words.

SELECTED READING LIST (POETRY)

ANTHOLOGIES

Deaf American Poetry, edited by John Lee Clarke, Gallaudet University Press, 2009

Beauty is a Verb: The New Poetry of Disability, edited by Sheila Black and Jennifer Bartlett, Cinco Puntos Press, 2011

Stairs and Whispers: D/deaf and Disabled Poets Write Back, edited by Sandra Alland, Khairani Barokka and Daniel Sluman, Nine Arches Press, 2017

Shaping the Fractured Self: Poetry of Chronic Illness and Pain, edited by Heather Taylor-Johnson, UWA, 2017

We Are Not Your Metaphor: a disability poetry anthology, Squares and Rebels, 2019 (featuring poems from Zoeglossia Fellows)

What Meets the Eye? The Deaf Perspective, edited by Lisa Kelly and Sophie Stone, Arachne Press, 2021

In Between Spaces: An Anthology of Disabled Writers, edited by Rebecca Burke, Stillhouse Press, 2022

The Ending Hasn't Happened Yet, edited by Hannah Soyer, Sable Books, 2022

Admissions: Voices within Mental Health, edited by David Stavanger, Radhiah Chowdhury and Mohammas Aswad, Upswell Poetry, 2022

Raging Grace: Australian Writers Speak Out on Disability, edited by Andy Jackson, Kerri Shying and Esther Ottaway, Puncher & Wattman, 2024

JOURNALS AND MAGAZINES, SPECIAL THEMED ISSUES AND FOLIOS

Southerly (Issue 76.2, 2016): 'Writing Disability', edited by David Brooks and Andy Jackson

Magma Poetry (Issue 69, Winter 2017), 'The Deaf Issue', edited by Lisa Kelly and Raymond Antrobus

Nat. Brut (Issue 11, Fall 2018): 'Beyond Resilience', edited by Kay Ulanday Barrett

Westerly Magazine (Online special issue 7, May 2019): 'DisAbility', edited by Josephine Taylor

Pandemic Artifacts / from the Zoomshell (a Turtle Disco Disability Culture Production, August 2021), edited by Stephanie Heit and Petra Kuppers

Modern Poetry in Translation (no.1, Spring 2022), 'The Fingers of Our Soul: The Bodies Focus' guest edited by Khairani Barokka and Jamie Hale

Contemporary Verse 2 (Vol. 44, Issue No. 4, Spring 2022) 'Sick Poetics', guest edited by Eileen Holowka, Rebecca Salazar and Lauren Turner

Poetry Wales (Vol. 58, No. 1, Summer 2022), guest edited by Hannah Hodgson

In-Na-Po in collaboration with Abalone Mountain Press, 'The Future Lives in Our Bodies: Indigeneity and Disability Justice', edited by Amber McCrary and Johnnie Jae

'Atlas: Skin/Bone/Blood – Bodymaps in Brown and Black: A Folio of Disabled Latinx Poetry', in *Apogee Journal* (2022), edited by heidi andrea restrepo rhodes

The Massachusetts Review (Vol. LXIII, No. 4, Winter 2022) 'Disability Justice', guest edited by Khairani Barokka and Cyrée Jarelle Johnson

Arc Poetry (Issue 102: Fall 2023) 'Disability Desirability', edited by Therese Estacion

Revista N'oj (Issue 6, Spring 2024) 'Disability Justice', edited by Quetzal Ruvalcaba

Pleiades (44.1: Spring 2024) 'On Disability', edited by Kennedy Horton and Olivia Ellisor

PUBLICATION ACKNOWLEDGEMENTS

The poems in this anthology are reprinted from the following books, journals and websites, all by permission of the publishers listed unless stated otherwise. Thanks are due to all the copyright holders cited below for their kind permission:

Iyanuoluwa Adenle: 'Beneath the Waves' from *Olongo Africa* (21 April 2021), by permission of the author. **Ekiwah Adler-Beléndez:** 'Evening Summer Rain' from *The Massachusetts Review*, 'Disability Justice' (Volume 63, No. 04, 2022), by permission of the author. **Agha Shahid Ali:** 'Not All, Only a Few Return' from *Call Me Ishmael: A Book of Ghazals* (W.W. Norton & Co., 2013). **Sandra Alland:** 'having been' from *Naturally Speaking* (espresso, Toronoto, 2012), by permission of the author. **Shahd Alshammari:** 'Injections' from *Forget the Words* (Dar Kalemat Publishing, Kuwait, 2016), by permission of the author. **JK Anowe:** 'a musical malady' from *Kissing Dynamite: A Journal of Poetry*, Issue 13, 2020, by permission of the author. **Raymond Antrobus:** 'For Tyrone Givans' from *All the Names Given* (Picador, 2021), by permission of David Higham Associates Ltd. **Dean Atta:** 'Five Litres of Blue' from *There is (still) love here* (Nine Arches Press, 2022). **Polly Atkin:** 'Breath Test' from *Much With Body* (Seren Books, 2021).

Urvashi Bahuguna: 'Medical History': https://scroll.in/article/910244/terrarium-five-poems-that-engage-with-the-complexities-of-health-with-vivid-originality. **Abdullah al-Baradouni:** 'Why I Am Silent about the Lament', tr. Threa Almontaser, from *The Wild Fox of Yemen* (Graywolf Press, US, 2021; Picador, UK, 2021), by permission of Pan Macmillan US. **Khairani Barokka:** 'Tub' from *amuk* (Nine Arches Press, 2024). **Kay Ulanday Barrett:** 'Sick 4 Sick' from *Zoeglossia* (April 2021) by permission of the author. **Levent Beşkardęş:** 'V' tr. Stephanie Papa from *Modern Poetry in Translation* (no.1 2022), by permission of the translator; the French version is a translation by Brigitte Baumié, J.Carlos Carreras, Guillaume Gigleux and Michel Thion of Levent Beşkardęş's signed poem, with the help of interpreters. It was published in the anthology

Les Mains Fertiles: 50 poètes en langue des signes (Éditions Bruno Doucey, 2015). **Brandi Bird:** 'Ode to Diabetes' from *The All + Flesh* (House of Anansi Press, 2023), © 2023 by Brandi Bird, by permission of House of Anansi Press, Toronto; www.houseofanansi.com. **Erez Bitton:** 'You Who Cross My Path', tr. Tsipi Keller, from *You Who Cross My Path: Selected Poems* (BOA Editions Ltd, 2015), copyright © 2009, 2013 by Erez Bitton; translation copyright © 2015 by Tsipi Keller; by permission of The Permissions Company, LLC on behalf of BOA Editions, Ltd., boaeditions.org. **Jean 'Binta' Breeze:** 'riddym ravings (the mad woman's poem)' from *Third World Girl: Selected Poems* (Bloodaxe Books, 2011). **Jane Burn:** 'An Evanescent Garden' from *The Apothecary of Flight* (Nine Arches Press, 2024). **Madailín Burnhope:** 'Camel Girl' from *A Miniature Book of Monsters* (unpublished manuscript) by permission of the author.

Jen Campbell: 'First Thing, I Am a Forest' from *Please Do Not Touch This Exhibit* (Bloodaxe Books, 2023). **Anthony Vahni Capildeo:** 'Plague Poems' from *Like a Tree, Walking* (Carcanet Press, 2021). **Paul Celan:** 'Afternoon with Circus and Citadel', tr. Michael Hamburger, from *Poems of Paul Celan* (Anvil Press Poetry, 2007), by permission of Carcanet Press Ltd. **Cat Chong:** '—I accept the task from the sun—' from *712 Stanza Homes for the Sun* (Broken Sleep Books, 2023). **John Lee Clarke:** 'At the Holiday Gas Station' from *How to Communicate: Poems* (W.W. Norton & Company), copyright © 2023 by John Lee Clarke, by permission of W. W. Norton & Company, Inc.

Kate Davis: 'Hand-writing practice' from *The Girl Who Forgets How to Walk* (Penned in the Margins, 2018). **Kwame Dawes:** 'Keratoconus' from *Sturge Town* (Peepal Tree Press, UK, 2023; W.W. Norton & Company, US, 2024). **Meg Day:** 'It Must Still Be Summer' from *Poetry Northwest* (Volume XVII, Issue 2, Winter & Spring 2023), by permission of the author. **Josephine Dickinson:** 'Alphabetula' from *Magma*, 'The Deaf Issue' (Issue 69, Winter 2017), also included, together with a short essay 'Notes on the poem Alphabetula', in *Aural Diversity*, ed. John Drever and Andrew Hugill (Routledge, 2023), by permission of the author.

Ali Cobby Eckermann: 'Kulila' from *Inside My Mother* (Giramondo Poets, 2015). **Anita Endrezze:** 'Song-Maker' from *Blue Ridge Journal*, by permission of the author. **Therese Estacion:** 'The ABG (Able-Bodied Gaze)' from *Phantompains* (Book*hug Press, Toronto, Canada, 2021).

Megan Fernandes: 'Letter to a Young Poet' from *I Do Everything I'm Told* (Tin House, Portland, Oregon, 2023). **Janet Frame:** 'I Take into My Arms More Than I Can Bear to Hold' from *Storms Will Tell: Selected Poems* (Bloodaxe Books, 2008).

Kathryn Gray: 'Bournemouth' from *Hollywood or Home* (Seren Books, 2023). **torrin a. greathouse:** 'Essay Fragment: Medical Model of Disability' from *Wound from the Mouth of a Wound* (Milkweed Editions, 2020), copyright © 2020 by torrin a. greathouse, by permission of The Permissions Company LLC on behalf of Milkweed Editions. **Ona Gritz:** 'No' from *Geode* (Main Street Rag, 2014), by permission of the author.

Golan Haji: from 'A Soldier in a Madhouse', tr. Stephen Watts, from *Scale of Injury* (Al Mutawassit, Milan, 2016), by permission of the author and translator. **Jamie Hale:** 'Fibrotic', from UCL website (Yale-UCL Poetry Prize), 2021, by permission of the author. **Kerry Hardie:** 'Flesh' from *The Silence Came Close* (The Gallery Press, 2006) and *Selected Poems* (Bloodaxe Books/The Gallery Press, 2011), by permission of The Gallery Press, Loughcrew, Oldcastle, Co. Meath, Ireland. **Maya Abu al-Hayyat:** 'You Can't' from *You Can Be the Last Leaf: Selected Poems*, tr. Fady Joudah (Milkweed Editions, 2022), copyright © 2006, 2012, 2016, 2021 by Maya Abu Al-Hayyat; translation copyright © 2022 by Fady Joudah; reprinted with permission of Milkweed Editions. milkweed.org. **Stephanie Heit:** 'ETC. THE RESISTANCE' from *Psych Murders* (Wayne State University Press, 2022), by permission of the author. **Selima Hill:** 'Snouts' from *I May Be Stupid But I'm Not That Stupid* (Bloodaxe Books, 2019). **Hannah Hodgson:** 'Dancing with a Doctor' from *163 Days* (Seren Books, 2022). **Linda Hogan:** 'When the Body' from *A History of Kindness* (Torrey House Press, 2020). **Mishka Hoosen:** 'What wasn't said to the doctor' from *Call it a difficult night* (Deep South, 2015), by permission of the author. **Cynthia Huntington:** 'The Rapture' from *The Radiant* (Four Ways Books, 2003), copyright © 2003 by Cynthia Huntington, by permission of The Permissions Company, LLC on behalf of Four Way Books, fourwaybooks.com

Shiki Itsuma: 'Loam', tr. John Newton Webb; the original poem 土壌 was published by 方向社 (Hokosha) in 志樹逸馬詩集 (Poems of Shiki Itsuma, 1960).

Andy Jackson: 'Song not for you' from *Human Looking* (Giramondo, 2022). **Cyrée Jarelle Johnson:** 'Now Let the Weeping Cease' from *Slingshot* (Nightboat Books, 2019). **Rachael Johnson:** 'You Tear Out My Tongue' from *My Body is an Ill-fitting Costume* (Abalone Mountain Press, 2023). **I.S. Jones:** 'Self-Portrait as the Blk Girl Becoming the Beast Everyone Thought She Was' from *Spells of My Name* (Newfound Press, 2021).

Ilya Kaminsky: 'That Map of Bone and Opened Valves' from *Deaf Republic* (Graywolf Press, US, 2019; Faber & Faber, UK, 2019). **Lisa Kelly:** 'Blackbird and Beethoven' from *The House of the Interpreter* (Carcanet Press, 2023). **Gayle Kennedy:** 'After Viewing the Carved Trees Exhibition' from *Red Room Poetry* by permission of the author. **Aaron Kent:** 'Scabies vs Predator' from *Griefs to last & other poems*, unpublished, by permission of the author. **Jane Kenyon:** 'Having It Out with Melancholy' from *Let Evening Come: Selected Poems* (Bloodaxe Books, UK, 2005) and *Collected Poems* (Graywolf Press, 2005), copyright © 2005 by The Estate of Jane Kenyon, by permission of The Permissions Company, LLC on behalf of Graywolf Press, graywolfpress.org. **Karl Knights:** 'A Field Guide to Stares' from *The Dark Horse* (Volume 42, 2020) by permission of the author. **Petra Kuppers:** 'Craniosacral Rhythms' from *Gut Botany* (Wayne State University Press, 2020) by permission of the author. **Stephen Kuusisto:** 'Night Seasons' from *Only Bread, Only Light* (Copper Canyon Press, 2000), copyright © 2010 by Stephen Kuusisto, by permission of The Permissions Company, LLC on behalf of Copper Canyon Press, coppercanyonpress.org.

Khando Langri: 'Medicine mantra for the road' from Source: *Yeshe: A Journal of Tibetan Literature, Arts and Humanities* (vol. 2, no. 1, 2022), by permission of the author. **Adrienne Leddy:** 'Erupture' from *Indigeneity and Disability Justice* (Abalone Mountain Press & InNaPo, 2022), by permission of the author. **Gwyneth Lewis:** 'Will I?' from *First Rain in Paradise* (Bloodaxe Books, 2025). **Joanne Limburg:** 'The Alice Case' from *The Autistic Alice* (Bloodaxe Books, 2017). **Ada Limón:** 'The Endlessness' from *The New Yorker* (11 September 2023, by permission of Massie & McQuilkin Literary Agents, New York. **Sarah Lubala:** '6 Errant Thoughts on Being a Refugee' from *A History of Disappearance* (Botsotso Publishing, Johannesburg, 2022), by permission of the author. **Roddy Lumsden:** 'Against Complaint' from *Third Wish Wasted* (Bloodaxe Books, 2009).

Osip Mandelstam: 'Having deprived me...', tr. Richard & Elizabeth McKane, from *The Moscow & Voronezh Notebooks* (Bloodaxe Books, 2003). **Jack Mapanje:** 'Skipping Without Ropes' from *The Last of the Sweet Bananas: New & Selected Poems* (Bloodaxe Books, 2004). **Airea D. Matthews:** 'Eviction' from *Bread and Circus* (Scribner, US, 2023; Picador, UK, 2023). **Lateef McLeod:** 'I Am Too Pretty for Some "Ugly Laws"' from *Whispers of Krip Love Shouts of Krip Revolution* (Poetic Matrix Press, 2020). **Erica Mena:** *from* 'Featherbone', from Featherbone (Ricochet Editions, 2015), by permission of the author. **Kei Miller:** 'The Subaltern Dreams of Big' from The Fight & The Fiddle (Furious Flower Poetry Center, 2023), by permission of David Higham Associates. **Leroy F. Moore Jr:** 'Disabled World Nation' by permission of the author. **Tito Rajarshi Mukhopadhyay:** 'Misfit' from *Disability Studies Quarterly*, Vol. 30 No. 1 (2010), by permission of the author. **Les Murray:** 'Dog Fox Field' from *Collected Poems* (Carcanet Press, 2012).

Karthika Naïr (& Marilyn Hacker): from 'A Different Distance' from *A Different Distance: a renga* (Milkweed Editions, 2021), by permission of the authors.

Chisom Okafor: 'In another life, I am twenty-two, gifted and curious' from *Isele Magazine* (15 September 2021), by permission of the author. **Frank Ormsby:** 'Once a Day' from 'The Parkinson's Poems' in *The Darkness of Snow* (Bloodaxe Books, 2017). **Naomi Ortiz:** 'Epicenter' from *Rituals for Climate Change* (Punctum Books, 2023).

Saleem Hue Penny: 'Tinniō' from https://www.anothernewcalligraphy. com/shp-tinnio.html, by permission of the author. **Lucia Perillo:** 'Shrike Tree' from *Time Will Clean the Carcass Bones: Selected and New Poems* (Copper Canyon Press, 2005), copyright © 2005 by Lucia Perillo, by permission of The Permissions Company, LLC on behalf of Copper Canyon Press, www.coppercanyonpress.org. **Pascale Petit:** 'Bac du Sauvage' from *Beast* (Bloodaxe Books, 2025). **Leah Lakshmi Piepzna-Samarasinha:** 'Crip fairy godmother' from *Tonguebreaker: Poems and Performance Texts* (Arsenal Pulp Press, 2019).

Nat Raha: '[subterranean / dreaming grace roots]' by permission of the author. **heidi andrea restrepo rhodes:** 'A Small Disunified Theory' from *Wet Sands: poetry exchanges* (Libromobile, 2022), by permission of the author.

G.N. Saibaba: 'A Sparrow in My Cell' from *Why Do You Fear My Way So Much: Poems and Letters from Prison* (Speaking Tiger Books, 2022). **Riyad al-Saleh al-Hussein:** 'The Sleeping Boy', tr. Ibtihal Rida Mahmood, from *A Bull in a Jungle*, published post-humously in 1983, reprinted from *Arablit Quarterly* (18 January 2018) by permission of the translator. **Badr Shakir al-Sayyab:** 'Rain Song', tr. Lena Jayyusi, from https://www. poemist.com/badr-shakir-al-sayyab/ rain-song, by permission of the translator. **Masaoka Shiki:** '1898 Summer', tr. Burton Watson, from *Selected Poems* (Columbia University Press, 2000). **Kerri Shying:** 'and bulbul means heart', from *Know Your Country* (Puncher & Wattmann, 2020), by permission of the author and publisher. **Daniel Sluman:** 'the beautiful', from *single window* (Nine Arches Press, 2021). **Gaele Sobott:** 'Exuviae' from *Disability Arts Online*, 2021, by permission of the author. **William Soutar:** 'The Room' from *Poems of William Soutar: A New Selection*, ed. W.R. Aitken (Scottish Academic Press, 1988).

Steffi Tad-y: 'Duplex Ukol Sa Utang Na Loob' from *From the Shoreline* (Gordon Hill Press, Guelph, Ontario, Canada, 2022). **Hoshino Tomihiro:** 'Chewing My Pen', tr. John Newton Webb, from *Modern Poetry in Translation* (No. 1 2022). The picture-poem (original title 筆を噛む) was first published in Hoshino's collection 花よりも小さく (Smaller than Flowers), published in 2003 by 偕成社 (Kaiseisha), copyright 星野富弘美術館 (Hoshino Tomihiro Museum of Art). **Hàn Mặc Tử:** 'Here in Vĩ Dạ Hamlet', tr. N.T Anh, from *Modern Poetry in Translation* (No.1 2023), by permission of the translator.

Nuala Watt: 'Disabled Person's Travel Card' from *The Department of Work and Pensions Assesses a Jade Fish* (Blue Diode, 2024), by permission of the author. **David Wheatley:** 'Dyspraxia Ode' from *Child Ballad* (Carcanet Press, 2023).

Yu Xiuhua: 'A Leaky Boat', tr. Fiona Sze-Lorrain, from *Moonlight Rests on My Left Palm: Poems & Essays by Yu Xiuhua* (Astra House, 2021), by permission of the translator and publisher.

Zuo You: 'Bluff', tr. Yi Zhe, from *The Massachusetts Review*, 'Disability Justice' (Volume 63, No. 04, 2022), by permission of the translator.

Every effort has been made to trace copyright holders of the poems published in this book. The editor and publisher apologise if anything has been included without permission or without the appropriate acknowledgement, and would be glad to be told of anyone who has not been consulted.

INDEX OF POETS & TRANSLATORS